The Food & Cooking of
Cambodia

The Food & Cooking of
Cambodia

Over 60 authentic recipes from an undiscovered cuisine,
all shown step by step in over 300 stunning photographs

Ghillie Başan

with photography by Martin Brigdale

southwater

This edition is published by Southwater, an imprint of Anness Publishing Ltd Hermes House, 88–89 Blackfriars Road, London SE1 8HA
tel. 020 7401 2077; fax 020 7633 9499
www.southwaterbooks.com
www.annesspublishing.com

If you would like to investigate using the images in this book for publishing, promotions or advertising, please visit our website www.practicalpictures.com for more information.

UK agent: The Manning Partnership Ltd, 6 The Old Dairy, Melcombe Road, Bath BA2 3LR; tel. 01225 478444; fax 01225 478440; sales@manning-partnership.co.uk

UK distributor: Grantham Book Services Ltd, Isaac Newton Way, Alma Park Industrial Estate, Grantham, Lincs NG31 9SD; tel. 01476 541080; fax 01476 541061; orders@gbs.tbs-ltd.co.uk

North American agent/distributor: National Book Network, 4501 Forbes Boulevard, Suite 200, Lanham, MD 20706; tel. 301 459 3366; fax 301 429 5746; www.nbnbooks.com

Australian agent/distributor: Pan Macmillan Australia, Level 18, St Martins Tower, 31 Market St, Sydney, NSW 2000; tel. 1300 135 113; fax 1300 135 103; customer.service@macmillan.com.au

New Zealand agent/distributor: David Bateman Ltd, 30 Tarndale Grove, Off Bush Road, Albany, Auckland; tel. (09) 415 7664; fax (09) 415 8892

Publisher: Joanna Lorenz
Senior Managing Editor: Conor Kilgallon
Project Editors: Doreen Gillon, Emma Clegg and Molly Perham
Photographer: Martin Brigdale
Home economists: Lucy McKelvie and Bridget Sargeson
Stylist: Helen Trent
Designer: Nigel Partridge
Cover Design: Anthony Cohen
Production Controller: Lee Sargent

ETHICAL TRADING POLICY
At Anness Publishing we believe that business should be conducted in an ethical and ecologically sustainable way, with respect for the environment and a proper regard to the replacement of the natural resources we employ.

As a publisher, we use a lot of wood pulp to make high-quality paper for printing, and that wood commonly comes from spruce trees. We are therefore currently growing more than 500,000 trees in two Scottish forest plantations near Aberdeen – Berrymoss (130 hectares/320 acres) and West Touxhill (125 hectares/305 acres). The forests we manage contain twice the number of trees employed each year in paper-making for our books.

Because of this ecological investment programme, you can have the reassurance of knowing that a tree is being cultivated on your behalf to naturally replace the materials used to make the book you are holding.

Our forestry programme is run in accordance with the UK Woodland Assurance Scheme (UKWAS) and will be certified by the internationally recognized Forest Stewardship Council (FSC). The FSC is a non-government organization dedicated to promoting responsible management of the world's forests. Certification ensures forests are managed in an environmentally sustainable and socially responsible basis. For further information about this scheme, go to www.annesspublishing.com/trees

1 3 5 7 9 10 8 6 4 2

© Anness Publishing Ltd 2007

Previously published as part of a larger volume, *The Food and Cooking of Vietnam & Cambodia*.

Main cover image shows Braised Black Pepper Pork with Ginger from page 43.

NOTES
Bracketed terms are intended for American readers. For all recipes, quantities are given in both metric and imperial measures and, where appropriate, in standard cups and spoons. Follow one set of measures, but not a mixture.

Standard spoon and cup measures are level. 1 tsp = 5ml, 1 tbsp = 15ml, 1 cup = 250ml/ 8fl oz. Australian standard tablespoons are 20ml. Australian readers should use 3 tsp in place of 1 tbsp for measuring small quantities. American pints are 16fl oz/ 2 cups. American readers should use 20fl oz/ 2.5 cups in place of 1 pint when measuring liquids.

Electric oven temperatures in this book are for conventional ovens. When using a fan oven, the temperature will probably need to be reduced by about 10–20°C/ 20–40°F. Since ovens vary, you should check with your manufacturer's instruction book for guidance.

The nutritional analysis given for each recipe is calculated per portion (i.e. serving or item), unless otherwise stated. If the recipe gives a range, such as Serves 4–6, then the nutritional analysis will be for the smaller portion size, i.e. 6 servings. Measurements for sodium do not include salt added to taste.

Medium (US large) eggs are used unless otherwise stated.

CONTENTS

CAMBODIA TODAY

For most of its recent history, Cambodia has been shut off from the rest of the world, but that has all changed. Today, it is open to tourists, foreign investors and international trade. It is one of the poorest countries in South-east Asia, but there is a will to rebuild and get on with living. The capital, Phnom Penh, has emerged from economic ruin and military occupation to become a captivating place to visit with a lively, international atmosphere. And no visitor should miss the stunning temples of Angkor, which are a mesmerizing blend of symmetry and spirituality. Not only do they display man's devotion to his gods, but they are the heart and soul of Cambodia as they represent a time when the Khmer empire was the greatest in South-east Asia. Many Cambodians make pilgrimages to the temples of Angkor, and tourists can explore them on foot, by bicycle, on the back of an elephant or view them from a helicopter.

To the Cambodians, their homeland is called Kampuchea, which is derived from the word *kambu-ja*, meaning "those born of Kambu", who was the mythical founder of the country. After years of conflict, many displaced Cambodians and refugees have now

Below: Rice sellers on the Tonlé Sap Lake, Cambodia.

returned to their homeland to start life anew in this moment of peace. With them they have brought fresh ideas and wealth accumulated in countries of the Western world which, combined with the UN influence and foreign aid, makes Cambodia an interesting place to be. In the countryside, the peasants still struggle to survive from fishing and rice growing, whereas cities like Phnom Penh and Siem Reap seem to be thriving. There are Western bars and restaurants, selling beers and pizzas, adjacent to Chinese and Cambodian restaurants selling deep-fried frogs' legs and noodles. Young urban Cambodians are into MTV and Western fashion, while the older generations cling to their traditions. But, most of all, in spite of the suffering that simmers beneath the surface of every family, the Cambodian people are unfailingly enthusiastic and friendly.

CAMBODIAN CUISINE

The cuisine of Cambodia is experiencing a revival. Restaurants serving traditional Khmer dishes are popular in the cities, as well as in Cambodian communities in Australia, France and America. There are also many restaurants and stalls selling Chinese, Thai or Vietnamese food, all of which play a part in the overall cuisine of the country. Although rice and fish are the staple foods,

Above: A Kreung woman in a krama scarf selling custard apples and bananas in Ban Lung, Rattankiri province.

Cambodia's culinary culture has been influenced by India, Thailand, China, France and Vietnam. As a result, there are many dishes that resemble these cuisines, especially that of Vietnam, with a strong emphasis on coconut milk, and spices and herbs, particularly garlic, ginger, lemon grass, chillies and coriander (cilantro). Cambodia also enjoys the French colonial legacy of fresh baguettes, ice cream, and coffee.

On the whole, Cambodian cuisine has served the needs of a peasant culture, partly due to the decades of severe destruction of the land and the people at hands of brutal regimes. But it should not be forgotten that the once mighty Khmer empire spread over large sections of Thailand, Laos and Vietnam as well as Cambodia and would have played a big role in influencing the court cuisine at Hue, a city in central Vietnam, so Cambodian dishes would also have influenced Vietnamese ones. unfailingly enthusiastic and friendly.

MARKETS

The markets of Cambodia are lively, colourful and atmospheric. They display the country's fish, livestock and agricultural produce, while the aroma of freshly cooked snacks wafts from the makeshift stalls and noodle shops. The countryside markets also offer a similar selection of livestock and wildlife, including endangered animals, such as bears, tigers and rhinos, sold for their

meat, paws, hides, hooves and penises. There is one market in the small town of Skuon, near Phnom Penh, that differs from all others as it features large, black, furry spiders. Bred in holes to the north of the town, the spiders are deep-fried for breakfast, lunch and supper. Cracked open like crab, the spiders are devoured by pulling the legs off and sucking out the flesh.

GEOGRAPHICAL INFLUENCES

Cambodia lies at the heart of Indochina, bordered by Laos and Thailand to the north, and Vietnam to the east. It is linked to Vietnam by the Mekong River, which unifies their culinary ingredients. The north-east of Cambodia is wild and mountainous, home to Cambodia's ethnic minorities and much of its wildlife, which includes Asian elephants, Asiatic wild dog, black gibbons, leopards, tigers and dugongs. Wild animals are also found in the dense jungles in the east, and in the Cardamom and Elephant Mountains in the south-west. A variety of bamboos and palms grow in these mountainous regions. The symbol of Cambodia is the sugar palm tree, which is used in construction, and in the production of medicine, wine and vinegar.

The country's rice bowl is in the Battambang region to the west, and extensive rice paddies are found in the central lowlands, where dry crops such as maize and tobacco are also grown. Vegetables, fruit and nuts grow in the central and southern lowlands, and salt is extracted from the sea near Kampot, on the Gulf of Thailand.

Water sources

The two most important geographical features in Cambodia are the Mekong River, which is almost 5km/3 miles wide in places, and the Tonlé Sap Lake. The largest lake in South-east Asia, the Tonlé Sap provides fish and irrigation water for almost half of Cambodia's population who live on the low-lying

Right: Women washing clothes on a floating village on the Tonlé Sap Lake in Cambodia.

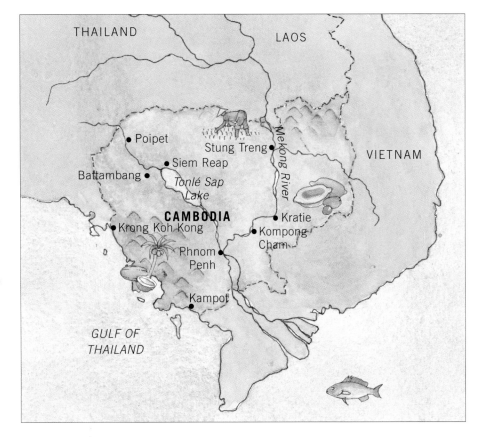

plain around lake and the upper Mekong Delta. The Tonlé Sap is linked to the Mekong by a 100km/60 mile channel, which is also called the Tonlé Sap. In the rainy season, when the level of the Mekong rises, the water backs up the channel causing it to flow into the lake, which swells up. When the water levels fall, it is drained back into the Mekong from the lake. This unusual process makes the lake one of the richest sources of freshwater fish in South-east Asia, and the flooded land is ideal for spawning.

CUSTOMS & FESTIVALS

On the whole, Cambodia is a very traditional society with an emphasis on strong family values and religion. The traditional greeting, the *sompiah*, involves pressing hands together in prayer and bowing. Generally, the higher the hand and the lower the bow, the more respect is shown. The culinary customs of Cambodia tend to be fairly relaxed. When eating at home, both the women and the men sit on floor mats with their feet to the side rather than in the lotus position. Traditionally, they followed the Hindu custom of using a hand to eat, but nowadays forks and chopsticks as well as hands are used.

CAMBODIAN MEALS

Most Cambodian dishes are cooked in a wok, known locally as a *chnang khteak*. For breakfast most Cambodians eat rice porridge, *bobor*, often with the addition of a little fish or pork. A traditional Cambodian meal almost always includes a soup, *samla*, which is eaten at the same time as the other courses. While rice is the country's staple, fish is the most important source of protein. Most of the fish eaten in Cambodia is freshwater, caught in the Tonlé Sap lake or Mekong River. Traditionally, fish is eaten wrapped in herbs and lettuce leaves and dipped in the national fish sauce *tuk trey*, which is similar to the Vietnamese *nuoc mam*.

FAMILY CELEBRATIONS

At weddings and festive banquets, there are a number of sweet snacks made in the home, or sold in the markets, such as sticky rice balls stuffed with banana, sticky rice cakes in banana leaves. and pumpkin pudding in banana leaves or *nom l'poh*.

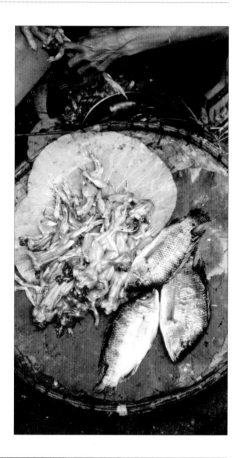

Right: Frogs and fish for sale at a stall on a street in Phnom Penh.

Below: Women making a communal meal around cooking pots and open fires in a typical village near Siem Riep.

FESTIVALS AND HOLIDAYS

The majority of Cambodians are followers of Theravada Buddhism, There are a number of religious festivals and national holidays, such as the Day for Remembering the Victory over the Genocidal Regime (7 January); the Chinese New Year, which usually falls around the same time as the Vietnamese *Tet*; the King's birthday; the Royal Ploughing Ceremony, *Chat Preah Nengkal*, held in early May in Phnom Penh to bless the farmers with successful crops in the coming year; and Independence Day on 9 November; the Khmer New Year; Buddha's birth, enlightenment and death; *Bon Om Tuk*; and Independence Day.

The Khmer New Year

Chaul Chnam, the Khmer New Year, lasts for three days in mid-April. Pilgrimages are made to the temples of Angkor and offerings are made at the temples and wats. Homes are cleaned out, gifts of new clothes are exchanged and food is shared. Water plays an important role in the celebrations as it

Below: A Khmer bride unwrapping the sacred coconut at a Buddhist wedding in Cambodia.

symbolizes cleansing and renewal. Religious statues are bathed in water and so is just about everyone else, as children and adults throw water missiles and fire water guns at anyone who goes by. Talcum powder missiles are also popular, spraying powder over people, cars and bicycles.

Above: Men rowing a long boat in the Retreat of the Waters during the Bon Om Tuk *festival in Phnom Penh.*

Bon Om Tuk

This is one of the most important festivals in Cambodia. Held in early November, it is a celebration of the reversal of the current of the Tonlé Sap. Just as the dry season begins, the water that is backed up in the lake begins to empty into the Tonlé Sap (the channel that links the lake to the Mekong) and on into the Mekong – a cause for much celebration. Boat races are held on the Tonlé Sap and on the moat around Angkor Wat.

Buddha's Birth, Enlightenment, and Death

Cambodia celebrates this event, which falls on the 15th day of the sixth lunar month. The festivities take place at pagodas and temples, which are decorated with lanterns and offerings of food. In the evening, a variety of processions take place – one of the most impressive is the candlelit procession of Buddhist monks at the ruins of Angkor Wat.

COOKING EQUIPMENT

The traditional Cambodian kitchen is basic. Often dark and sparsely kitted out with an open hearth, very little equipment is needed. Food is generally bought daily from the markets, taken home and cooked immediately so, unless you visit the kitchen during the frenzied moments of passionate activity over the hearth, there is little evidence of food or cooking. Without refrigerators, this reliance on fresh produce from the daily markets is vital. For some, two visits to the market are required – in the morning for the ingredients to cook for lunch, and, in the afternoon for the evening meal. Back in the simple kitchen, the activity always begins with the scrubbing of vegetables, the plucking and jointing of birds (if this hasn't been done in the markets), the endless chopping and slicing, and the pounding of herbs and spices with a pestle and mortar.

WOK

The wok is the most important utensil for everyday cooking in Cambodia. Everybody has one. Without a doubt, there is always something delicious being stir-fried in a home or in the streets. However, woks are not only used for stir-frying, they are also used for steaming, deep-frying, braising and soup-making. The most functional, multi-purpose wok should measure approximately 35cm/14in across, large enough for a family meal or to steam a whole fish. The most common wok is double-handled and made of lightweight carbonized steel. This is ideal for deep-frying and steaming but, for stir-frying, you need the single-handled version.

When you first buy a wok, you need to season it before use. Put it over a high heat to blacken the inside – this burns off any dust and factory coating. Leave the wok to cool, then immerse it in hot, soapy water and clean it with an abrasive cloth or stiff brush. Rinse it well and dry over a medium heat. Pour a little cooking oil into the base and, using a piece of kitchen paper, wipe it all around the surface of the wok. Now the wok is ready for use.

After each use, clean the wok with hot water only, dry it over a medium heat, and wipe a thin layer of oil over the surface. This will ensure that it doesn't get rusty. Over time, the wok

Above: A solid mortar and pestle is an essential piece of kitchen equipment.

will acquire a seasoned look – dark and glossy – and should last a lifetime. Woks are sold in all Chinese and Asian markets.

MORTAR AND PESTLE

A big mortar and pestle, made of stone, is of particular value, as it is used not only for grinding spices, chillies and garlic, but also for pounding all the condiments and pastes, as well as the meat for pâtés and savoury balls. Some cooks have several mortar and pestle sets, varying in size according to the activity and ingredient. Coffee grinders and electric blenders can be used as substitutes, but they don't release the oils and flavours of the ingredients in the same way and they produce too smooth a texture. It is worth looking for a solid stone mortar and pestle in Asian markets and kitchen suppliers.

BAMBOO STEAMER

Traditional bamboo steamers come in various sizes. The most practical one is about 30cm/12in wide, as it can be used for rice or a whole fish. Generally, the steamer is set directly over a wok that is filled with boiling water to below the level of the steamer. The food is placed in the steamer, either on a plate, or wrapped in muslin (cheesecloth), or banana leaves. The lid is placed on the steamer and, as the water in the wok is heated, the steam rises under and around the food, cooking it gently. A stainless steel steamer is no substitute

Left: A single-handed wok is good for stir-frying on the hob.

for a bamboo one, which imparts its own delicate fragrance to the dish. Bamboo steamers are available in most Asian stores and some cooking equipment suppliers.

CLAY POT

Made from a combination of light-coloured clay and sand, these pots come in all sizes, with single or double handles, lids, and glazed interiors. Perhaps the oldest form of cooking vessel, these attractive pots are ideal for slow-cooking, such as braised dishes and soups, as they retain an overall even heat. Generally, they are used on the stove over a low or medium heat, as a high temperature could cause them to crack. When you first
buy a clay pot, it needs to be treated for cooking. Fill it with water and place it over a low flame. Gradually increase the heat and let the water boil until it is reduced by half.

Right: Bamboo steamers come in several sizes.

Above: A clay pot can be used in the oven or, with care, on the stove.

Rinse the pot and dry thoroughly. Now it is ready for use. Traditional clay pots are available in some Asian markets.

CLEAVERS

Asian cleavers are the most important tools in the kitchen. There are special blades for the fine chopping of lemon grass and green papaya, heavy blades for opening coconuts, thin ones for shredding spring onions (scallions), and multi-purpose ones for any type of chopping, slicing and crushing. Generally, you use the front, lighter part of the blade for the regular chopping, slicing and shredding;

the back, heavier section is for chopping with force through bones; and the flat side is ideal for crushing ginger and garlic, and for transporting the ingredients into the wok.

draining spoon
Traditional draining spoons are made of wire with a long bamboo handle; more modern ones are made of perforated stainless steel. Both are flat and useful for deep-frying, for blanching noodles and for scooping ingredients out of hot liquid.

Left: Bamboo chopsticks are essential kitchen equipment.

Right: A medium-weight cleaver is a multi-purpose tool.

Right: Draining spoons are useful for deep-frying and blanching.

COOKING TECHNIQUES

The traditional cooking methods of Cambodia require few culinary tools but do need a great deal of attention to detail. Fresh ingredients are of the utmost importance, followed by the balance of sharp or mild, salty or sweet, bitter or sour, or a combination of all of these flavours. The layering of ingredients is also important, especially in Cambodian noodle dishes, where flavours and textures should complement each other but remain separate. Almost every meal is prepared from scratch, starting with the plucking of chickens and grinding of spices, followed by the grilling over charcoal, gentle simmering and steaming, or stir-frying. Armed with the correct equipment, the cooking is fairly easy – most of the work is in the preparation.

Grinding and pounding

Spices, herbs and other ingredients are usually ground and pounded in a large, heavy mortar made of stone. The interior of the mortar should be rough to grip the ingredients and act as an abrasive. The pestle needs to be heavy too, made of the same stone, to provide the right weight for pounding and grinding.

Grinding is most efficient if the herbs, spices and other ingredients are added in the correct order. First the hard seeds or nuts are ground together, then the fresh herbs, ginger and garlic, followed by the oils or pastes. The mixture is then bound and seasoned and ready for use.

DRY-FRYING

Dried spices are often roasted before grinding to release their natural oils and enhance the aroma. This is done by spreading the spices thinly in a heavy frying pan and putting it over a high heat. As the pan begins to heat, shake it so that the spices don't get too brown. Once the spices begin to colour and their aroma fills the air, put them in a mortar and grind to a powder.

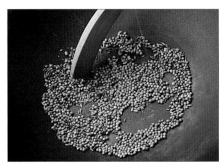

BRAISING

The classic method for slow-cooked dishes is braising. Generally, oily fish, duck and red meat are cooked this way, often with pungent herbs, spices and coconut milk or juice. Traditionally, to seal in the moisture, a covered clay pot is used as the cooking vessel. Placed over a medium heat, or in the oven, the cooking process can take anything from 30 minutes to 2 hours, depending on the dish. If you don't have a clay pot, use a heavy-based casserole. The key is in containing the moisture and even heat distribution, so don't use a thin aluminium pot.

1 Put all the ingredients in a clay pot and place in a preheated oven. (It can also be placed over a medium heat on the stove if you prefer.)

GRILLING OVER CHARCOAL

As conventional grills (broilers) don't exist in most homes in Cambodia, grilling is generally done over hot charcoal. This traditional method of cooking not only lends itself to many types of food, it also enhances the taste. Whole fish, pigs or chickens can be cooked this way. Tasty, marinated morsels of food, skewered on bamboo sticks and grilled in the streets, make popular snacks. When cooking over charcoal, light the coals and wait until they have turned red with grey or white ashes. If the charcoal is too hot, the food will just burn.

STEAMING

This is a popular way of preparing delicate-tasting foods, such as fish and shellfish, the French-inspired pork pâtés, as well as sticky rice cakes wrapped in banana or bamboo leaves. Place the food in a bamboo steamer, which should be lined with leaves if the food isn't wrapped in them. Put the lid on the steamer and set it over a wok that is half-filled with water. Bring the water to the boil, then reduce the heat and steam the food according to the recipe.

STIR-FRYING

Of all the cooking techniques, this is by far the most important one in Cambodia. The technique is more linked to the preparation of ingredients than the cooking process, which only takes minutes. Generally, the ingredients should be cut or shredded into bitesize morsels and laid out in the order in which they are to be cooked. To stir-fry successfully you need a wok, placed over a high heat, and a ladle or spatula to toss the ingredients around, so that they cook but still retain their freshness and crunchy texture.

1 Pour a little oil into the wok and place it over a high heat until hot.

2 Add the spices and aromatics to the oil and toss them around thoroughly to flavour the oil.

3 Add the pieces of meat or fish, and toss them in the wok for a minute or two.

4 Add the prepared root vegetables or mushrooms and stir-fry for a minute.

5 Add the leafy vegetables or beansprouts and toss them around quickly in the wok.

6 Toss in the herbs and seasonings and serve the stir-fry. The key is to work quickly and layer the ingredients according to the time they require for cooking.

7 Serve hot straight from the wok into warmed bowls and don't leave the food sitting in the wok.

DEEP-FRYING

Use an oil that can be heated to a high temperature, such as groundnut (peanut) oil, and don't put in too much cold food at once, as this will cool the oil down.

1 Pour the oil into a pan or wok (filling it no more than two-thirds full) and heat to about 180°C/350°F. To test the temperature, add a drop of batter or a piece of onion. If it sinks, the oil is not hot enough; if it burns, it is too hot. If it sizzles and rises to the surface, the temperature is perfect.

2 Cook the food in small batches until crisp and lift out with a slotted spoon or wire mesh skimmer when cooked.

3 Drain on a wire rack lined with kitchen paper and serve immediately, or keep warm in the oven until you are ready to serve.

BLANCHING

This method is often used to cook delicate meat such as chicken breast portions or duck.

1 Place the meat and any flavourings in a pan and add just enough water to cover. Bring to the boil, then remove from the heat and leave to stand, covered, for 10 minutes, then drain.

Prahoc

This popular fish-based condiment is an essential component of Cambodian cooking. Extremely pungent, it is made by fermenting whole fish, or chunks of fish, with ground rice and salt. Once added to dishes, it mellows in odour and enhances the flavour of the other ingredients. Jars of *prahoc* are available in Asian stores.

Making tuk prahoc

Generally, *prahoc* is not used from the jar; a small amount is diluted in boiling water and strained – this is called *tuk prahoc*, used in practically every Cambodian savoury dish.

In a pan, bring 250ml/8fl oz/1 cup water to the boil. Reduce the heat and add roughly 30ml/2 tbsp of *prahoc*. Simmer gently for 10 minutes, until the fish has broken down and the water is cloudy. Strain the fish through a sieve set over a bowl to extract the liquid, pressing down on the fish. Strain the liquid again, through a piece of muslin (cheesecloth), to make sure it is running clear. Leave to cool and store in an airtight container in a cool place.

SOUPS & SAVOURY SNACKS

Almost all Cambodian meals will have soup as an accompaniment, ranging from Hot-and-sour Fish Soup to Duck and Preserved Lime Soup, and these are served with the main meal, rather than as an appetizer. Soup is also a popular breakfast dish, and is served as a snack throughout the day. Snacks on the go or at home are an integral part of daily life in Cambodia, and choices range from Crunchy Summer Rolls to Fried Squid with Salt and Pepper.

SPICY TOMATO AND EGG DROP SOUP

POPULAR AMONG THE CHINESE COMMUNITIES IN CAMBODIA, THIS SPICY SOUP WITH EGGS IS PROBABLY ADAPTED FROM THE TRADITIONAL CHINESE EGG DROP SOUP. SERVED ON ITS OWN WITH CHUNKS OF CRUSTY BREAD, OR ACCOMPANIED BY JASMINE OR GINGER RICE, THIS IS PERFECT FOR A LIGHT SUPPER.

SERVES FOUR

INGREDIENTS
   30ml/2 tbsp groundnut (peanut) or
     vegetable oil
   3 shallots, finely sliced
   2 garlic cloves, finely chopped
   2 Thai chillies, seeded and
     finely sliced
   25g/1oz galangal, shredded
   8 large, ripe tomatoes, skinned,
     seeded and finely chopped
   15ml/1 tbsp sugar
   30ml/2 tbsp *tuk trey*
   4 lime leaves
   900ml/1½ pints/3¾ cups
     chicken stock
   15ml/1 tbsp wine vinegar
   4 eggs
   sea salt and ground black pepper
For the garnish
   chilli oil, for drizzling
   1 small bunch fresh coriander
     (cilantro), finely chopped
   1 small bunch fresh mint leaves,
     finely chopped

2 Just before serving, bring a wide pan of water to the boil. Add the vinegar and half a teaspoon of salt. Break the eggs into individual cups or small bowls.

3 Stir the water rapidly to create a swirl and drop an egg into the centre of the swirl. Follow immediately with the others, or poach two at a time, and keep the water boiling to throw the whites up over the yolks. Turn off the heat, cover the pan and leave to poach until firm enough to lift. Poached eggs are traditional, but you could use lightly fried eggs instead.

4 Using a slotted spoon, lift the eggs out of the water and slip them into the hot soup. Drizzle a little chilli oil over the eggs, sprinkle with the coriander and mint, and serve.

1 Heat the oil in a wok or heavy pan. Stir in the shallots, garlic, chillies and galangal and cook until golden and fragrant. Add the tomatoes with the sugar, *tuk trey* and lime leaves. Stir until it resembles a sauce. Pour in the stock and bring to the boil. Reduce the heat and simmer for 30 minutes. Season.

VARIATION
The soup is very tasty without the eggs and could be served as a spicy tomato soup on its own.

Per portion Energy 181Kcal/756kJ; Protein 8g; Carbohydrate 12.3g, of which sugars 11.5g; Fat 11.7g, of which saturates 2.4g; Cholesterol 190mg; Calcium 52mg; Fibre 2.3g; Sodium 280g

CRUNCHY SUMMER ROLLS

THESE DELIGHTFUL RICE PAPER ROLLS FILLED WITH CRUNCHY RAW SUMMER VEGETABLES AND FRESH HERBS ARE LIGHT AND REFRESHING, AND ARE EATEN EITHER AS A SNACK OR AN APPETIZER TO A MEAL. THE ROLLS ARE ENJOYED THROUGHOUT CAMBODIA.

SERVES FOUR

INGREDIENTS
    12 round rice papers
    1 lettuce, leaves separated and
    ribs removed
    2–3 carrots, cut into julienne strips
    1 small cucumber, peeled, halved
    lengthways and seeded, and cut
    into julienne strips
    3 spring onions (scallions), trimmed
    and cut into julienne strips
    225g/8oz mung beansprouts
    1 bunch fresh mint leaves
    1 bunch coriander (cilantro) leaves
    dipping sauce, to serve
    (see Cook's Tips)

1 Pour some lukewarm water into a shallow dish. Then soak the rice papers, 2–3 at a time, for about 5 minutes until they are pliable. Place the soaked papers on a clean dishtowel and then cover with a second dishtowel to keep them moist.

2 Work with one paper at a time. Place a lettuce leaf towards the edge nearest to you, leaving about 2.5cm/1in to fold over. Place a mixture of the vegetables on top, followed by some mint and coriander leaves.

VARIATION

This recipe only uses vegetables, which are cut into equal lengths, but you can also add pre-cooked shredded pork, chicken or prawns to summer rolls.

3 Fold the edge nearest to you over the filling, tuck in the sides, and roll tightly to the edge on the far side. Place the filled roll on a plate and cover with clear film (plastic wrap), so it doesn't dry out.

4 Repeat with the remaining rice papers and vegetables. Serve with a dipping sauce of your choice. If you are making these summer rolls ahead of time, keep them in the refrigerator under a damp dishtowel, so that they remain moist.

COOK'S TIPS
• In Cambodia, these crunchy filled rolls are accompanied by a dipping sauce called *tuk trey*. They are also delicious when accompanied with any kind of dipping sauce.
• The rice papers, in which these rolls are wrapped, can be bought in Chinese and South-east Asian markets.

Per portion 106Kcal/445kJ; Protein 3.5g; Carbohydrate 21.2g, of which sugars 4.7g; Fat 0.7g, of which saturates 0.2g; Cholesterol 0mg; Calcium 44mg; Fibre 2.2g; Sodium 10mg

CURRIED SWEET POTATO BALLS

These sweet potato balls from Cambodia are delicious dipped in a fiery sauce, such as tuk trey, fried black chilli sauce or hot peanut dipping sauce. Incredibly simple to make, they are ideal for serving as a nibble with a drink.

2 Pull off lumps of the dough and mould them into small balls – you should be able to make roughly 24 balls. Roll the balls on a bed of sesame seeds or poppy seeds until they are completely coated.

3 Heat enough oil for deep-frying in a wok. Fry the sweet potato balls in batches, until golden. Drain on kitchen paper. Serve the balls with wooden skewers to make it easier to dip them into a dipping sauce of your choice.

SERVES FOUR

INGREDIENTS
    450g/1lb sweet potatoes or taro root, boiled or baked, and peeled
    30ml/2 tbsp sugar
    15ml/1 tbsp Indian curry powder
    25g/1oz fresh root ginger, peeled and grated
    150g/5oz/1¼ cups glutinous rice flour or plain (all-purpose) flour
    salt
    sesame seeds or poppy seeds
    vegetable oil, for deep-frying
    dipping sauce, to serve

1 In a bowl, mash the cooked sweet potatoes or taro root. Beat in the sugar, curry powder, and ginger. Add the rice flour (sift it if you are using plain flour) and salt, and work into a stiff dough – add more flour if necessary.

Per portion Energy 354Kcal/1495kJ; Protein 5g; Carbohydrate 61g, of which sugars 14.8g; Fat 11.8g, of which saturates 1.5g; Cholesterol 0mg; Calcium 84mg; Fibre 3.9g; Sodium 50mg

HOT-AND-SOUR FISH SOUP

THIS TANGY SOUP, SAMLAW M'JUU TREY, IS FOUND THROUGHOUT SOUTH-EAST ASIA — WITH THE BALANCE OF HOT, SWEET AND SOUR FLAVOURS DEPENDING ON THE REGION. CHILLIES PROVIDE THE HEAT, TAMARIND PRODUCES THE TARTNESS AND THE DELICIOUS SWEETNESS COMES FROM PINEAPPLE.

SERVES FOUR

INGREDIENTS

1 catfish, sea bass or red snapper, about 1kg/2¼lb, filleted
30ml/2 tbsp *tuk prahoc*
2 garlic cloves, finely chopped
25g/1oz dried squid, soaked in water for 30 minutes
15ml/1 tbsp vegetable oil
2 spring onions (scallions), sliced
2 shallots, sliced
4cm/1½in fresh root ginger, peeled and chopped
2–3 lemon grass stalks, cut into strips and crushed
30ml/2 tbsp tamarind paste
2–3 Thai chillies, seeded and sliced
15ml/1 tbsp sugar
30–45ml/2–3 tbsp *nuoc mam*
225g/8oz fresh pineapple, peeled and diced
3 tomatoes, skinned, seeded and roughly chopped
50g/2oz canned sliced bamboo shoots, drained
1 small bunch fresh coriander (cilantro), stalks removed, leaves finely chopped
salt and ground black pepper
115g/4oz/½ cup beansprouts and 1 bunch dill, fronds roughly chopped, to garnish
1 lime, cut into quarters, to serve

1 Cut the fish into bitesize pieces, mix with the *tuk prahoc* and garlic and leave to marinate. Save the head, tail and bones for the stock. Drain and rinse the soaked dried squid.

2 Heat the oil in a deep pan and stir in the spring onions, shallots, ginger, lemon grass and dried squid. Add the reserved fish head, tail and bones, and sauté them gently for a minute or two. Pour in 1.2 litres/2 pints/5 cups water and bring to the boil. Reduce the heat and simmer for 30 minutes.

3 Strain the stock into another deep pan and bring to the boil. Stir in the tamarind paste, chillies, sugar and *tuk prahoc* and simmer for 2–3 minutes. Add the pineapple, tomatoes and bamboo shoots and simmer for a further 2–3 minutes. Stir in the fish pieces and the chopped fresh coriander, and cook until the fish turns opaque.

4 Season to taste with salt and pepper and ladle the soup into hot bowls. Garnish with beansprouts and dill, and then serve with the lime quarters to squeeze over.

VARIATIONS

• Depending on your mood, or your palate, you can adjust the balance of hot and sour by adding more chilli or tamarind to taste. Enjoyed as a meal in itself, the soup is usually served with plain steamed rice or with chunks of fresh bread, which are perfect for soaking up the spicy, fruity, tangy broth.
• Other fresh herbs, such as chopped mint and basil leaves, also complement this soup.

Per portion Energy 335Kcal/1415kJ; Protein 44g; Carbohydrate 24g, of which sugars 19g; Fat 7g, of which saturates 1g; Cholesterol 108mg; Calcium 138mg; Fibre 2.3g; Sodium 1.2g

FRIED SQUID WITH SALT AND PEPPER

COOKING SQUID COULDN'T BE SIMPLER. SALT AND PEPPER ARE USED TO SEASON, AND THAT'S IT. A CHINESE TRADITION FOR ALL SORTS OF FISH AND SHELLFISH, THIS IS A CAMBODIAN FAVOURITE TOO. IDEAL SNACK AND FINGER FOOD, THE TENDER SQUID CAN BE SERVED ON ITS OWN.

SERVES FOUR

INGREDIENTS
  450g/1lb baby or medium squid
  30ml/2 tbsp coarse salt
  15ml/1 tbsp ground black pepper
  50g/2oz/½ cup rice flour or
    cornflour (cornstarch)
  vegetable oil, for deep-frying
  2 limes, halved

1 Prepare the squid by pulling the head away from the body. Sever the tentacles from the rest and trim them. Reach inside the body sac and pull out the backbone, then clean the squid inside and out, removing any skin. Rinse well in cold water.

2 Using a sharp knife, slice the squid into rings and pat them dry with kitchen paper. Put them in a dish with the tentacles. Combine the salt and pepper with the rice flour or cornflour, add it to the squid and toss well, making sure it is evenly coated.

3 Heat the oil for deep-frying in a wok or heavy pan. Cook the squid in batches, until the rings turn crisp and golden. Drain on kitchen paper and serve with limes to squeeze over. This dish can also be served with noodles, or with chunks of baguette and fresh chillies.

Per portion Energy 339Kcal/1405kJ; Protein 14g; Carbohydrate 5g, of which sugars 0g; Fat 29g, of which saturates 4g; Cholesterol 146mg; Calcium 70mg; Fibre 0g; Sodium 140mg

BAMBOO, FISH AND RICE SOUP

THIS IS A REFRESHING KHMER SOUP MADE WITH FRESHWATER FISH. A SPECIALITY OF PHNOM PENH,
SAMLAW TRAPEANG IS FLAVOURED WITH COCONUT MILK, THE FERMENTED FISH EXTRACT, TUK
PRAHOC, LEMON GRASS AND GALANGAL — SOME OF CAMBODIA'S PRINCIPAL INGREDIENTS.

SERVES FOUR

INGREDIENTS
  75g/3oz/scant ½ cup long grain rice,
    well rinsed
  250ml/8fl oz/1 cup coconut milk
  30ml/2 tbsp *tuk prahoc*
  2 lemon grass stalks, trimmed
    and crushed
  25g/1oz galangal, thinly sliced
  2–3 Thai chillies
  4 garlic cloves, crushed
  15ml/1 tbsp palm sugar
  1 fresh bamboo shoot, peeled,
    boiled in water for 10 minutes,
    and sliced
  450g/1lb freshwater fish fillets,
    such as carp or catfish, skinned
    and cut into bitesize pieces
  1 small bunch fresh basil leaves
  1 small bunch fresh coriander
    (cilantro), chopped, and 1 chilli,
    finely sliced, to garnish
  rice or noodles, to serve
For the stock
  675g/1½lb pork ribs
  1 onion, quartered
  225g/8oz carrots, cut into chunks
  25g/1oz dried squid or dried shrimp,
    soaked in water for 30 minutes,
    rinsed and drained
  15ml/1 tbsp *tuk trey*
  15ml/1 tbsp soy sauce
  6 black peppercorns
  salt

1 To prepare the stock, put the ribs in a large pan and cover with 2.5 litres/ 4¼ pints/10 cups water. Bring to the boil, skim off any fat, and add the remaining stock ingredients. Cover the pan and simmer for 1 hour, then skim off any foam or fat.

2 Simmer the stock, uncovered, for a further 1–1½ hours, until it has reduced. Check the seasoning and strain the stock into another pan. There should be approximately 2 litres/3½ pints/7¾ cups of stock.

3 Bring the pan of stock to the boil. Stir in the rice and reduce the heat. Add the coconut milk, *tuk prahoc*, lemon grass, galangal, chillies, garlic and sugar. Simmer for about 10 minutes to let the flavours mingle. The rice should be just cooked, with bite to it.

4 Add the sliced bamboo shoot and the pieces of fish. Simmer for 5 minutes, until the fish is cooked. Check the seasoning and stir in the basil leaves. Ladle the soup into bowls, garnish with the chopped coriander and chilli, and serve with the rice or noodles.

Per portion Energy 181Kcal/763kJ; Protein 22.8g; Carbohydrate 19.6g, of which sugars 4.3g; Fat 1.3g, of which saturates 0.2g; Cholesterol 52mg; Calcium 64mg; Fibre 0.9g; Sodium 150mg

DEEP-FRIED PRAWN SANDWICHES

IN THE BUSY STREET MARKETS OF PHNOM PENH, THERE IS ALWAYS SOMETHING INTERESTING BEING COOKED. NEXT TO THE STALL SELLING DEEP-FRIED FURRY, BLACK SPIDERS, YOU MIGHT COME ACROSS THE LESS ALARMING SNACK OF DEEP-FRIED PRAWN SANDWICHES.

SERVES FOUR

INGREDIENTS
    3–4 shallots, roughly chopped
    4 garlic cloves, roughly chopped
    25g/1oz fresh root ginger, peeled
      and chopped
    1 lemon grass stalk, trimmed
      and chopped
    1 Thai chilli, seeded and chopped
    10ml/2 tsp sugar
    225g/8oz fresh prawns (shrimp),
      shelled and deveined
    30ml/2 tbsp *tuk trey*
    1 egg, beaten
    12 thin slices of day-old baguette
    vegetable oil, for deep-frying
    ground black pepper
    chilli oil, for drizzling

1 Using a large mortar and pestle, pound the chopped shallots, garlic, ginger, lemon grass, chilli and sugar. Add the shelled prawns and pound them too to make a paste. Mix well and bind all the ingredients with the *tuk trey* and beaten egg. Season with ground black pepper.

2 Spread the mixture on each piece of bread, patting it down firmly. In a wok, heat enough oil for deep-frying. Using a slotted spoon, lower the sandwiches, prawn side down, into the oil. Cook in batches, flipping them over so they turn golden on both sides. Drain on kitchen paper and serve hot with chilli oil.

Per portion Energy 489Kcal/2065kJ; Protein 22.5g; Carbohydrate 70.6g, of which sugars 6.3g; Fat 15g, of which saturates 2g; Cholesterol 157mg; Calcium 202mg; Fibre 3.1g; Sodium 860mg

GRILLED PRAWNS <u>WITH</u> LEMON GRASS

NEXT TO EVERY FISH STALL IN EVERY MARKET IN CAMBODIA, THERE IS BOUND TO BE SOMEONE COOKING UP FRAGRANT, CITRUS-SCENTED SNACKS FOR YOU TO EAT AS YOU WANDER AROUND THE MARKET. THE AROMATIC SCENT OF LEMON GRASS IS HARD TO RESIST.

SERVES FOUR

INGREDIENTS

16 king prawns (jumbo shrimp),
  cleaned, with shells intact
120ml/4fl oz/½ cup *tuk trey*
30ml/2 tbsp sugar
15ml/1 tbsp vegetable or sesame oil
3 lemon grass stalks, trimmed and
  finely chopped

3 Pour the marinade over the prawns, using your fingers to rub it all over the prawns and inside the shells too. Cover the dish with clear film (plastic wrap) and chill for at least 4 hours.

4 Cook the prawns on a barbecue or under a conventional grill (broiler) for 2–3 minutes each side. Serve with little bowls of water for rinsing sticky fingers.

1 Using a small sharp knife, carefully slice open each king prawn shell along the back and pull out the black vein, using the point of the knife. Try to keep the rest of the shell intact. Place the deveined prawns in a shallow dish and set aside.

2 Put the *tuk trey* in a small bowl with the sugar, and beat together until the sugar has dissolved completely. Add the oil and lemon grass and mix well.

COOK'S TIP
Big, juicy king prawns (jumbo shrimp) are best for this recipe, but you can use smaller ones if the large king prawns are not available.

Per portion Energy 174Kcal/726kJ; Protein 13g; Carbohydrate 11g, of which sugars 3g; Fat 9g, of which saturates 1g; Cholesterol 169mg; Calcium 30mg; Fibre 0.3g; Sodium 30mg

DRY-COOKED PORK STRIPS

THIS CAMBODIAN DISH IS QUICK AND LIGHT ON A HOT DAY. PORK, CHICKEN, PRAWNS AND SQUID CAN ALL BE COOKED THIS WAY. WITH THE LETTUCE AND HERBS, IT'S A VERY FLAVOURSOME SNACK, BUT YOU CAN SERVE IT WITH A DIPPING SAUCE, IF YOU LIKE.

SERVES TWO TO FOUR

INGREDIENTS

   15ml/1 tbsp groundnut (peanut) oil
   30ml/2 tbsp *tuk trey*
   30ml/2 tbsp soy sauce
   5ml/1 tsp sugar
   225g/8oz pork fillet, cut into thin,
     bitesize strips
   8 lettuce leaves
   chilli oil, for drizzling
   fresh coriander (cilantro) leaves
   a handful of fresh mint leaves

VARIATION

Try basil, flat leaf parsley, spring onions or sliced red onion in these parcels.

1 In a wok or heavy pan, heat the oil, *tuk trey* and soy sauce with the sugar. Add the pork and stir-fry over a medium heat, until all the liquid has evaporated. Cook the pork until it turns brown, almost caramelized, but not burnt.

2 Drop spoonfuls of the cooked pork into lettuce leaves, drizzle a little chilli oil over the top, add a few coriander and mint leaves, wrap them up and serve immediately.

Per portion Energy 96Kcal/401kJ; Protein 12.2g; Carbohydrate 0.4g, of which sugars 0.4g; Fat 5g, of which saturates 1.1g; Cholesterol 35mg; Calcium 7mg; Fibre 0.1g; Sodium 300mg

DUCK AND PRESERVED LIME SOUP

THIS RICH CAMBODIAN SOUP, SAMLAW TIAH, ORIGINATES IN THE CHIU CHOW REGION OF SOUTHERN CHINA. THIS RECIPE CAN BE MADE WITH CHICKEN STOCK AND LEFTOVER DUCK MEAT FROM A ROASTED DUCK, OR BY ROASTING A DUCK, SLICING OFF THE BREAST AND THIGH MEAT FOR THE SOUP.

SERVES FOUR TO SIX

INGREDIENTS
    1 lean duck, approximately
        1.5kg/3lb 5oz
    2 preserved limes
    25g/1oz fresh root ginger,
        thinly sliced
    sea salt and ground black pepper
For the garnish
    vegetable oil, for frying
    25g/1oz fresh root ginger,
        thinly sliced into strips
    2 garlic cloves, thinly sliced
        into strips
    2 spring onions (scallions),
        finely sliced

COOK'S TIPS
• With the addition of noodles, this soup could be served as a meal in itself.
• Preserved limes have a distinct bitter flavour. Look for them in Asian markets.

1 Place the duck in a large pan with enough water to cover. Season with salt and pepper and bring the water to the boil. Reduce the heat, cover the pot, and simmer for 1½ hours.

2 Add the preserved limes and ginger. Continue to simmer for another hour, skimming off the fat from time to time, until the liquid has reduced a little and the duck is so tender that it almost falls off the bone.

3 Meanwhile heat some vegetable oil in a wok. Stir in the ginger and garlic strips and fry until gold and crispy. Drain well on kitchen paper and set aside for garnishing.

4 Remove the duck from the broth and shred the meat into individual bowls. Check the broth for seasoning, then ladle it over the duck in the bowls. Scatter the spring onions with the fried ginger and garlic over the top and serve.

Per portion Energy 124Kcal/520kJ; Protein 19.8g; Carbohydrate 0.3g, of which sugars 0.3g; Fat 6.5g, of which saturates 1.3g; Cholesterol 110mg; Calcium 19mg; Fibre 0g; Sodium 100mg

SPICY BEEF AND AUBERGINE SOUP

A WONDERFUL KHMER DISH, THIS SOUP, SAMLAW MACHOU KROEUNG, IS SWEET, SPICY AND TANGY. THE FLAVOUR IS MAINLY DERIVED FROM THE CAMBODIAN HERBAL CONDIMENT, KROEUNG, AS WELL AS THE FERMENTED FISH EXTRACT, TUK TREY.

SERVES SIX

INGREDIENTS
    4 dried New Mexico chillies
    15ml/1 tbsp vegetable oil
    75ml/5 tbsp *kroeung*
    2–3 fresh or dried red Thai chillies
    75ml/5 tbsp tamarind extract
    15–30ml/1–2 tbsp *tuk trey*
    30ml/2 tbsp palm sugar
    12 Thai aubergines (eggplants), with
       stems removed and cut into
       bitesize chunks
    1 bunch watercress or rocket
       (arugula), trimmed and chopped
    1 handful fresh curry leaves
    sea salt and ground black pepper
For the stock
    1kg/2¼ lb beef shanks or brisket
    2 large onions, quartered
    2–3 carrots, cut into chunks
    90g/3½ oz fresh root ginger, sliced
    2 cinnamon sticks
    4 star anise
    5ml/1 tsp black peppercorns
    30ml/2 tbsp soy sauce
    45–60ml/3–4 tbsp *tuk trey*

2 Soak the New Mexico chillies in water for 30 minutes. Split them open, remove the seeds and scrape out the pulp with a spoon.

3 Take the lid off the stock and stir in the remaining two ingredients. Simmer, uncovered, for another hour, until the stock has reduced to about 2 litres/3½ pints/7¾ cups. Skim off any fat, strain the stock into a bowl and put aside. Lift the meat on to a plate, tear it into thin strips and put half of it aside for the soup.

6 Meanwhile, dry-fry the curry leaves. Heat a small, heavy pan over a high heat, add the curry leaves and cook them until they begin to crackle. Transfer them to a plate and set aside.

7 Season the soup to taste. Stir in half the curry leaves and ladle the soup into individual bowls. Scatter the remaining curry leaves over the top and serve.

1 To make the stock, put the beef shanks into a deep pan with all the other stock ingredients, apart from the soy sauce and *tuk trey*. Cover with 3 litres/5 pints/12 cups water and bring it to the boil. Reduce the heat and simmer, covered, for 2–3 hours.

COOK'S TIP
For a greater depth of flavour, you can dry-roast the New Mexico chillies before soaking them in water.

4 Heat the oil in a wok or heavy pan. Stir in the *kroeung* along with the pulp from the New Mexico chillies and the whole Thai chillies. Stir the spicy paste as it sizzles, until it begins to darken. Add the tamarind extract, *tuk trey*, sugar and the reserved stock. Stir well and bring to the boil.

5 Reduce the heat and add the reserved beef, aubergines and watercress or rocket. Continue cooking for about 20 minutes to allow the flavours to mingle.

Per portion Energy 303Kcal/1276kJ; Protein 37g; Carbohydrate 16.5g, of which sugars 14.5g; Fat 10.6g, of which saturates 4.2g; Cholesterol 90mg; Calcium 35mg; Fibre 2.4g; Sodium 300mg

FISH & SHELLFISH

Cambodia's huge lake, the Tonlé Sap, and its many rivers including the Mekong, mean that the country enjoys an abundance of saltwater and freshwater fish and shellfish. Trey aing, or grilled fish, and trey chean neung spey, or fried fish with vegetables, are widely available. Coconut milk is often used to prepare fish, such as Sea Bass Steamed in Coconut Milk with Ginger, Cashew Nuts and Basil, or try a taste of the forest with Jungle Fish Cooked in Banana Leaves.

JUNGLE FISH COOKED ᴵᴺ BANANA LEAVES

STEAMING FRESHWATER FISH IN BANANA LEAVES OVER HOT CHARCOAL IS A TRADITIONAL METHOD OF COOKING IN THE JUNGLE. BANANA LEAVES ARE LARGE AND TOUGH, AND SERVE AS BASIC COOKING VESSELS AND WRAPPERS FOR ALL SORTS OF FISH AND MEAT.

SERVES FOUR

INGREDIENTS
  350g/12oz freshwater fish fillets,
    such as trout, cut into
    bitesize chunks
  6 banana leaves
  vegetable oil, for brushing
  sticky rice, noodles or salad, to serve
For the marinade
  2 shallots
  5cm/2in turmeric root, peeled
    and grated
  2 spring onions (scallions),
    finely sliced
  2 garlic cloves, crushed
  1–2 green Thai chillies, seeded
    and finely chopped
  15ml/1 tbsp *tuk trey*
  2.5ml/½ tsp raw cane sugar
  salt and ground black pepper

1 To make the marinade, grate the shallots into a bowl, then combine with the other marinade ingredients, Season with salt and pepper. Toss the chunks of fish in the marinade, then cover and chill for 6 hours, or overnight.

VARIATION
This dish can be made with any of the catfish or carp family, or even talapia.

2 Prepare a barbecue. Place one of the banana leaves on a flat surface and brush it with oil. Place the marinated fish on the banana leaf, spreading it out evenly, then fold over the sides to form an envelope. Place this envelope, fold side down, on top of another leaf and fold that one in the same manner. Repeat with the remaining leaves until they are all used up.

3 Secure the last layer of banana leaf with a piece of bendy wire. Place the banana leaf packet on the barbecue. Cook for about 20 minutes, turning it over from time to time to make sure it is cooked on both sides – the outer leaves will burn. Carefully untie the wire (it will be hot) and unravel the packet. Check that the fish is cooked and serve with sticky rice, noodles or salad.

COOK'S TIP
Banana leaves are available in some African and Asian stores and markets. If you can't find them, wrap the fish in vine leaves that have been soaked in cold water, or large flexible cabbage leaves. You can also use foil.

Per portion Energy 155Kcal/648kJ; Protein 18g; Carbohydrate 4g, of which sugars 2g; Fat 8g, of which saturates 1g; Cholesterol 59mg; Calcium 36mg; Fibre 0.7g; Sodium 200mg

FISH IN COCONUT CUSTARD

THIS IS A KHMER CLASSIC. RICH AND SUMPTUOUS, AMOK TREY CROPS UP ALL OVER CAMBODIA. IN PHNOM PENH, THERE ARE RESTAURANTS THAT SPECIALIZE IN IT. THE FISH IS STEAMED IN A CUSTARD, MADE WITH COCONUT MILK AND FLAVOURED WITH THE CAMBODIAN HERBAL PASTE, KROEUNG.

SERVES FOUR

INGREDIENTS
   2 x 400ml/14oz cans coconut milk
   3 eggs
   80ml/3fl oz *kroeung*
   15ml/1 tbsp *tuk trey*
   10ml/2 tsp palm sugar or honey
   1 kg/2¼lb fresh, skinned white fish
      fillets, cut into 8 pieces
   1 small bunch chopped fresh
      coriander (cilantro), plus a few
      whole sprigs, to garnish
   jasmine rice or crusty bread and
      salad, to serve

VARIATION
If you don't have a big enough steamer, this dish can be cooked in the oven in a bain marie. Cook at 160°C/325°F/Gas 3 for about 50 minutes.

1 Half fill a wok or large pan with water. Set a bamboo or stainless steel steamer over it and put the lid on. Bring the water to the boil.

2 In a bowl, beat the coconut milk with the eggs, *kroeung, tuk trey* and sugar or honey, until it is well blended and the sugar has dissolved.

3 Place the fish fillets in a heatproof dish that will fit in the steamer. Pour the coconut mixture over the fish and place the dish in the steamer. Put the lid back on the steamer and reduce the heat so that the custard won't curdle. Steam over gently simmering water until the fish is cooked. Garnish with coriander and serve immediately with jasmine rice or crusty bread and salad.

Per portion Energy 309Kcal/1304kJ; Protein 51.1g; Carbohydrate 12.4g, of which sugars 12.4g; Fat 6.5g, of which saturates 1.8g; Cholesterol 258mg; Calcium 103mg; Fibre 0g; Sodium 400mg

SEA BASS STEAMED <u>IN</u> COCONUT MILK <u>WITH</u> GINGER, CASHEW NUTS <u>AND</u> BASIL

THIS IS A DELICIOUS RECIPE FOR ANY WHOLE WHITE FISH, SUCH AS SEA BASS OR COD, OR FOR LARGE CHUNKS OF TROUT OR SALMON. YOU WILL NEED A STEAMER LARGE ENOUGH TO FIT THE WHOLE FISH OR, IF USING FISH CHUNKS, YOU CAN USE A SMALLER STEAMER AND FIT THE FISH AROUND THE BASE.

SERVES FOUR

INGREDIENTS
    200ml/7fl oz coconut milk
    10ml/2 tsp raw cane or muscovado
      (molasses) sugar
    about 15ml/1 tbsp vegetable oil
    2 garlic cloves, finely chopped
    1 red Thai chilli, seeded and
      finely chopped
    4cm/1½in fresh root ginger, peeled
      and grated
    750g/1lb 10oz sea bass, gutted and
      skinned on one side
    1 star anise, ground
    1 bunch fresh basil, stalks removed
    30ml/2 tbsp cashew nuts
    sea salt and ground black pepper
    rice and salad, to serve

1 Heat the coconut milk with the sugar in a small pan, stirring until the sugar dissolves, then remove from the heat. Heat the oil in a small frying pan and stir in the garlic, chilli and ginger. Cook until they begin to brown, then add the mixture to the coconut milk and mix well to combine.

2 Place the fish, skin side down, on a wide piece of foil and tuck up the sides to form a boat-shaped container. Using a sharp knife, cut several diagonal slashes into the flesh on the top and rub with the ground star anise. Season with salt and pepper and spoon the coconut milk over the top, making sure that the fish is well coated.

3 Scatter half the basil leaves over the top of the fish and pull the foil packet almost closed. Lay the packet in a steamer. Cover the steamer, bring the water to the boil, reduce the heat and simmer for 20–25 minutes, or until just cooked. Alternatively, place the foil packet on a baking tray and cook in a preheated oven at 180°C/350°F/Gas 4.

4 Roast the cashew nuts in the frying pan, adding extra oil if necessary. Drain the nuts on kitchen paper, then grind them to crumbs. When the fish is cooked, lift it out of the foil and transfer it to a serving dish. Spoon the cooking juices over, sprinkle with the cashew nut crumbs and garnish with the remaining basil leaves. Serve with rice and a salad.

Per portion Energy 235Kcal/983kJ; Protein 26g; Carbohydrate 8g, of which sugars 6g; Fat 11g, of which saturates 2g; Cholesterol 100mg; Calcium 217mg; Fibre 0.3g; Sodium 300mg

CHARCOAL-GRILLED FISH <u>WITH</u> CHILLI <u>AND</u> GINGER SAUCE

A WHOLE FISH GRILLED OVER CHARCOAL IS KNOWN AS TREI AING AND IT IS USUALLY SERVED WITH SALAD LEAVES, HERBS, CHOPPED PEANUTS, AND A STRONG-FLAVOURED SAUCE. CHUNKS OF THE COOKED FISH ARE WRAPPED IN THE LEAVES AND DIPPED IN THE SAUCE.

SERVES TWO TO FOUR

INGREDIENTS

  1 good-sized fish, such as trout, snakehead, barb or carp, gutted and rinsed, head removed, if you like
  225g/8oz mung beansprouts
  1 bunch each fresh basil, coriander (cilantro) and mint, stalks removed, leaves chopped
  1 lettuce, broken into leaves
  30ml/2 tbsp roasted unsalted peanuts, finely chopped
  steamed rice, to serve
For the sauce
  3 garlic cloves, chopped
  2 red Thai chillies, seeded and chopped
  25g/1oz fresh root ginger, peeled and chopped
  15ml/1 tbsp palm sugar
  45ml/3 tbsp *tuk trey*
  juice of 1 lime
  juice of 1 coconut

1 First prepare the sauce. Using a mortar and pestle, grind the garlic, chillies and ginger with the sugar to form a paste. Add the *tuk trey*, lime juice and coconut juice and bind well. Pour the sauce into a serving bowl.

2 Prepare the barbecue. Place the fish over the charcoal and grill it for 2–3 minutes each side, until cooked right through. Alternatively, use a conventional grill (broiler).

3 Lay out the beansprouts, herbs and lettuce leaves on a large plate and place the peanuts in a bowl. Put everything in on the table, including the cooked fish, sauce and rice. Using chopsticks, if you like, lift up the charred skin and tear off pieces of fish. Place each piece on a lettuce leaf, sprinkle with beansprouts, herbs and peanuts, wrap it up and dip it into the sauce.

Per portion Energy 231Kcal/971kJ; Protein 41.2g; Carbohydrate 4.1g, of which sugars 2.5g; Fat 5.6g, of which saturates 0.9g; Cholesterol 92mg; Calcium 101mg; Fibre 3g; Sodium 130mg

Baby Squid Stuffed with Pork, Mushrooms, Tiger Lily Buds and Dill

Popular among the Chinese and Vietnamese communities in Cambodia, squid is generally stir-fried or stuffed. This recipe calls for the tender baby squid to be stuffed with a dill-flavoured pork mixture. The squid can be grilled or fried.

SERVES FOUR

INGREDIENTS
3 dried cloud ear (wood ear)
   mushrooms
10 dried tiger lily buds
25g/1oz bean thread
   (cellophane) noodles
8 baby squid
350g/12oz minced (ground) pork
3–4 shallots, finely chopped
4 garlic cloves, finely chopped
1 bunch dill fronds, finely chopped
30ml/2 tbsp *tuk trey*
5ml/1 tsp palm sugar
ground black pepper
vegetable or groundnut (peanut) oil,
   for frying
coriander (cilantro) leaves, to garnish
tuk trey dipping sauce, for drizzling

2 Meanwhile, prepare the squid one at a time. Hold the body sac in one hand, hold the head with the other and pull it off. Pull out the backbone and rinse out the body sac. Peel off the outer membrane, pat the body sac dry, and put aside. Sever the tentacles from the head. Discard the head and chop the tentacles. Repeat with the other squid.

4 In a small bowl, stir the *tuk trey* dipping sauce with the sugar, until it dissolves completely. Add it to the mixture in the bowl and mix well. Season with ground black pepper.

5 Using your fingers, stuff the pork mixture into each squid, packing it in firmly. Leave a little gap at the end to sew together with a needle and cotton thread or to skewer with a cocktail stick (toothpick) so that the filling doesn't spill out on cooking.

1 Soak the mushrooms, tiger lily buds and bean thread noodles in lukewarm water for about 15 minutes, until they have softened.

3 Drain the soaked tree ear mushrooms, tiger lily buds and bean thread noodles. Squeeze them in kitchen paper to get rid of any excess water, then chop them finely and put them in a bowl. Add the chopped tentacles, minced pork, shallots, garlic and three-quarters of the dill. Mix well.

COOK'S TIPS
• Instead of frying the squid, you can cook them over a charcoal or conventional grill (broiler).
• Served on a platter, these baby squid are an impressive sight at parties.

6 Heat some oil in a large wok or heavy pan, and fry the squid for about 5 minutes, turning them from time to time. Pierce each one several times to release any excess water – this will cause the oil to spit, so take care when doing this; you may wish to use a spatterproof lid. Continue cooking for a further 10 minutes, until the squid are nicely browned. Serve whole or thinly sliced, garnished with the remaining dill and coriander and *tuk trey* dipping sauce.

Per portion Energy 315Kcal/1311kJ; Protein 25g; Carbohydrate 7.9g, of which sugars 1.9g; Fat 20.4g, of which saturates 4.6g; Cholesterol 170mg; Calcium 18mg; Fibre 0.2g; Sodium 110mg

SOUR CARP <u>WITH</u> TAMARIND <u>AND</u> GALANGAL

THIS RIVER CARP DISH IS POPULAR IN BOTH CAMBODIA AND VIETNAM. IF YOU WOULD RATHER MAKE A SLIGHTLY SIMPLER VERSION OF THE SAME DISH, YOU COULD JUST TOSS THE COOKED FISH IN THE HERBS AND SERVE IT WITH NOODLES OR RICE AND A SALAD.

4 Heat a wok or heavy pan, add the sesame or vegetable oil and then stir in the turmeric. Working quickly, so the turmeric doesn't burn, add the fish pieces, gently moving them around the wok for 2–3 minutes.

5 Add any remaining marinade to the pan and cook for a further 2–3 minutes, or until the pieces of fish are cooked through.

SERVES FOUR

INGREDIENTS
500g/1¼lb carp fillets, cut into 3
 or 4 pieces
30ml/2 tbsp sesame or vegetable oil
10ml/2 tsp ground turmeric
1 small bunch each fresh coriander
 (cilantro) and basil, stalks removed
20 lettuce leaves or rice wrappers
tuk trey or other dipping sauce,
 to serve
For the marinade
30ml/2 tbsp tamarind paste
15ml/1 tbsp soy sauce
juice of 1 lime
1 green or red Thai chilli,
 finely chopped
2.5cm/1in galangal root, peeled
 and grated
a few sprigs of fresh coriander
 (cilantro) leaves, finely chopped

1 Prepare the marinade by mixing together all the marinade ingredients.

2 Toss the pieces of carp fillet in the marinade, cover the bowl with clear film (plastic wrap) and chill in the refrigerator for a minimum of 6 hours, or overnight.

3 Lift the pieces of fish out of the marinade and lay them on a plate.

6 To serve, divide the fish among four plates, sprinkle with the coriander and basil, and add some of the lettuce leaves or rice wrappers and a small bowl of dipping sauce to each serving. To eat, tear off a bitesize piece of fish, place it on a wrapper with a few herb leaves, fold it up into a roll, then dip it into the sauce.

COOK'S TIP
Any freshwater fish can be used for this recipe but, because it is stirred in a wok, you will need one with firm, thick flesh, such as catfish or barb. Allow plenty of time for the fish to marinate and soak up the flavours.

Per portion Energy 298Kcal/1246kJ; Protein 24g; Carbohydrate 19g, of which sugars 5g; Fat 14g, of which saturates 2g; Cholesterol 121mg; Calcium 120mg; Fibre 0g; Sodium 300mg

CATFISH COOKED IN A CLAY POT

WONDERFULLY EASY AND TASTY, THIS CAMBODIAN DISH IS A CLASSIC. CLAY POTS ARE REGULARLY USED FOR COOKING AND THEY ENHANCE BOTH THE LOOK AND TASTE OF THIS TRADITIONAL DISH. VARY THE RECIPE BY ADDING CHILLIES AND OTHER GREENS.

SERVES FOUR

INGREDIENTS

- 30ml/2 tbsp sugar
- 15ml/1 tbsp sesame or vegetable oil
- 2 garlic cloves, crushed
- 45ml/3 tbsp *tuk trey*
- 350g/12oz catfish fillets, cut diagonally into 2 or 3 pieces
- 4 spring onions (scallions), cut into bitesize pieces
- ground black pepper
- chopped fresh coriander (cilantro), to garnish
- fresh bread, to serve

3 Remove the lid, season with ground black pepper and gently stir in the spring onions. Simmer for a further 3–4 minutes to thicken the sauce, garnish with fresh coriander, and serve immediately straight from the pot with chunks of fresh bread.

1 Place the sugar in a clay pot or heavy pan, and add 15ml/1 tbsp water to wet it. Heat the sugar until it begins to turn golden brown, then add the oil and crushed garlic.

2 Stir the *tuk trey* into the caramel mixture and add 120ml/4fl oz/½ cup boiling water, then toss in the catfish pieces, making sure they are well coated with the sauce. Cover the pot, reduce the heat and simmer for about 5 minutes.

Per portion Energy 126Kcal/533kJ; Protein 16g; Carbohydrate 10g, of which sugars 8g; Fat 3g, of which saturates 0g; Cholesterol 40mg; Calcium 25mg; Fibre 0.2g; Sodium 600mg

MEAT, POULTRY & FROG'S LEGS

Beef, pork, chicken, duck and other poultry are used in dishes throughout Cambodia, although they are more expensive and therefore seen as more luxurious ingredients than fish. Pork is the principal meat, with many rural families keeping a pig, and every bit is put to good use — as the Stewed Caramelized Pig's Feet, with its rich, velvety sauce, testifies. Popular throughout the region, frogs are sold live in markets and recipes include Stir-fried Frog's Legs with its fragrant kroeung *sauce.*

STIR-FRIED BEEF <u>WITH</u> SESAME SAUCE

THIS DISH IS A REAL STAPLE OF THE REGION, AND VARIATIONS CAN BE FOUND ALL OVER CAMBODIA. SIMILAR TO STIR-FRIED BEEF WITH SATÉ, THE SPICY PEANUT SAUCE, THIS RECIPE HAS A DELICIOUSLY RICH, SPICY AND NUTTY FLAVOUR.

<u>SERVES FOUR</u>

INGREDIENTS
  450g/1lb beef sirloin or fillet,
    cut into thin strips
  15ml/1 tbsp groundnut (peanut)
    or sesame oil
  2 garlic cloves, finely chopped
  2 red Thai chillies, seeded and
    finely chopped
  7.5ml/1½ tsp sugar
  30ml/2 tbsp sesame paste
  30–45ml/2–3 tbsp beef stock
    or water
  sea salt and ground black pepper
  red chilli strips, to garnish
  1 lemon, cut into quarters, to serve
For the marinade
  15ml/1 tbsp groundnut (peanut) oil
  30ml/2 tbsp *tuk trey*
  30ml/2 tbsp soy sauce

1 In a bowl, mix together the ingredients for the marinade. Toss in the beef, making sure it is well coated. Leave to marinate for 30 minutes.

2 Heat the groundnut or sesame oil in a wok or heavy pan. Stir in the garlic and chillies and cook until golden and fragrant. Stir in the sugar. Add the beef, tossing it around the wok to sear it.

3 Stir in the sesame paste and enough stock or water to thin it down. Cook for 1–2 minutes, making sure the beef is coated with the sauce. Season with salt and pepper, garnish with chilli strips and and serve with lemon wedges.

VARIATION
Chicken breast fillet or pork fillet can be used instead of beef.

Per portion Energy 269Kcal/1119kJ; Protein 26.2g; Carbohydrate 2/0g, of which sugars 2.0g; Fat 18g, of which saturates 5g; Cholesterol 65mg; Calcium 31mg; Fibre 0.3g; Sodium 73mg

SEARED GARLIC BEEF DIPPED IN LIME JUICE

VARIATIONS OF THIS DISH ARE POPULAR THROUGHOUT SOUTHEAST ASIA. IN THIS CAMBODIAN VERSION, THE TENDER CHUNKS OF BEEF ARE WRAPPED IN LETTUCE LEAVES AND DIPPED IN A PIQUANT LIME SAUCE. THE BEEF CAN BE SEARED IN A PAN, OR CHARGRILLED.

SERVES FOUR

INGREDIENTS

   350g/12oz beef fillet or sirloin, cut
      into bitesize chunks
   15ml/1 tbsp sugar
   juice of 3 limes
   2 garlic cloves, crushed
   7.5ml/1½ tsp ground black pepper
   30ml/2 tbsp unsalted roasted
      peanuts, finely chopped
   12 lettuce leaves
For the marinade
   15ml/1 tbsp groundnut (peanut) oil
   45ml/3 tbsp mushroom soy sauce
   10ml/2 tsp soy sauce
   15ml/1 tbsp sugar
   2 garlic cloves, crushed
   7.5ml/1½ tsp ground black pepper

2 In a small bowl, stir the sugar into the lime juice, until it has dissolved. Add the garlic and black pepper and beat well. Stir in the peanuts and put aside.

3 Heat a wok or heavy pan and sear the meat on all sides. Serve immediately with lettuce leaves for wrapping and the lime sauce for dipping.

1 To make the marinade, beat together the oil, the two soy sauces and the sugar in a bowl, until the sugar has dissolved. Add the garlic and pepper and mix well. Add the beef and coat in the marinade. Leave for 1–2 hours.

Per portion Energy 237Kcal/986kJ; Protein 22g; Carbohydrate 5.2g, of which sugars 4.7g; Fat 14g, of which saturates 4g; Cholesterol 51mg; Calcium 12mg; Fibre 0.5g; Sodium 324mg

MINCED MEAT WITH CHARRED AUBERGINE

VARIATIONS OF THIS DISH CROP UP IN DIFFERENT PARTS OF SOUTH-EAST ASIA. TO ATTAIN THE UNIQUE, SMOKY FLAVOUR, THE AUBERGINES ARE CHARRED OVER A FLAME, OR CHARCOAL GRILL, THEN SKINNED, CHOPPED TO A PULP AND ADDED TO THE DISH.

SERVES FOUR

INGREDIENTS

   2 aubergines (eggplants)
   15ml/1 tbsp vegetable or groundnut
     (peanut) oil
   2 shallots, finely chopped
   4 garlic cloves, peeled and
     finely chopped
   1 red Thai chilli, finely chopped
   350g/12oz minced (ground) beef
   30ml/2 tbsp *tuk trey*
   sea salt and ground black pepper
   crusty bread or rice and salad,
     to serve

VARIATION
This dish can also be made with beef or pork – either way it is delicious served with chunks of fresh, crusty bread.

1 Place the aubergines directly over an open flame. Turn them over from time to time, until the skin is charred all over. Put the aubergines into a plastic bag to sweat for a few minutes.

2 Hold each aubergine by its stalk under running cold water, while you peel off the skin. Squeeze out the excess water and chop them roughly on a board.

3 Heat the oil in a large, heavy pan. Stir in the shallots, garlic and chilli and fry until golden. Add the minced beef and stir-fry for about 5 minutes.

4 Stir in the *tuk trey* and the aubergine and cook gently for about 20 minutes, until the meat is tender. Season with salt and pepper and serve with crusty bread or rice and a salad.

Per portion Energy 245Kcal/1019kJ; Protein 19g; Carbohydrate 4g, of which sugars 3.4g; Fat 17g, of which saturates 6g; Cholesterol 53mg; Calcium 23mg; Fibre 2.2g; Sodium 607mg

BRAISED BLACK PEPPER PORK WITH GINGER

ADAPTED FROM A RECIPE BY CORINNE TRANG, THIS CAMBODIAN DISH IS QUICK, TASTY AND BEAUTIFULLY WARMING THANKS TO THE ADDITION OF GINGER AND BLACK PEPPER. THIS IS SURE TO BE A POPULAR CHOICE FOR A FAMILY MEAL.

SERVES FOUR TO SIX

INGREDIENTS

   1 litre/1¾ pints/4 cups pork stock
     or water
   45ml/3 tbsp *tuk trey*
   30ml/2 tbsp soy sauce
   15ml/1 tbsp sugar
   4 garlic cloves, crushed
   40g/1½oz fresh root ginger, peeled
     and finely shredded
   15ml/1 tbsp ground black pepper
   675g/1½lb pork shoulder or rump,
     cut into bitesize cubes
   steamed jasmine rice, crunchy salad
     and pickles or stir-fried greens,
     such as water spinach or long
     beans, to serve

1 In a large heavy pan, bring the stock or water, *tuk trey* and the soy sauce to the boil. Then reduce the heat and stir in the sugar, garlic, ginger, black pepper and pork.

2 Cover the pan and simmer for about 1½ hours, until the pork is very tender and the liquid has reduced. Serve the pork with a fresh crunchy salad, pickles, or stir-fried greens.

Per portion Energy 147Kcal/619kJ; Protein 24g; Carbohydrate 2.7g, of which sugars 2.7g; Fat 4g, of which saturates 2g; Cholesterol 71mg; Calcium 11mg; Fibre 0.1g; Sodium 81mg

GRILLED PORK MEATBALLS WITH SWEET-AND-SOUR PEANUT SAUCE

VARIATIONS OF THESE MEATBALLS ARE COOKED THROUGHOUT SOUTH-EAST ASIA, AT HOME OR IN STREET STALLS. IN CAMBODIA, THEY ARE TRADITIONALLY SERVED WITH A FIERY PEANUT DIPPING SAUCE OR THE NATIONAL TUK TREY DIPPING SAUCE, OR CHOPPED CORIANDER AND LIME WEDGES.

SERVES FOUR

INGREDIENTS
10ml/2 tsp groundnut (peanut) or
   sesame oil
4 shallots, chopped
2 garlic cloves, finely chopped
450g/1lb/2 cups minced
   (ground) pork
30ml/2 tbsp *tuk trey*
10ml/2 tsp five-spice powder
10ml/2 tsp sugar
115g/4oz/2 cups breadcrumbs or
   30ml/2 tbsp potato starch
1 bunch fresh coriander (cilantro),
   stalks removed
salt and ground black pepper
For the sauce
10ml/2 tsp groundnut (peanut) oil
1 garlic clove, finely chopped
2–3 red Thai chillis, seeded and
   finely chopped
30ml/2 tbsp roasted peanuts,
   finely chopped
15ml/1 tbsp *tuk trey*
30ml/2 tbsp rice wine vinegar
30ml/2 tbsp hoisin sauce
60ml/4 tbsp coconut milk
100ml/3½fl oz/scant ½ cup water
5ml/1 tsp sugar

VARIATION
These meatballs can be threaded on to skewers and grilled on a barbecue, or they can be cooked under a grill (broiler), fried in a wok or steamed.

COOK'S TIP
Adding breadcrumbs makes the paste considerably easier to work with and doesn't then interfere with the meaty texture of the cooked ball. Some cooks tend to prefer potato starch to breadcrumbs, because it gives the meatball a smooth, springy texture, although this does also make the paste very sticky to handle. Work with wet hands to make it easier.

1 To make the sauce, heat the oil in a small wok or heavy pan, and stir in the garlic and chilli. When they begin to colour, add the peanuts. Stir-fry for a few minutes, or until the natural oil from the peanuts begins to weep. Add the remaining ingredients, except the sugar, and boil the mixture for a minute. Adjust the sweetness and seasoning to your taste by adding sugar and salt, and set aside.

2 To make the meatballs, heat the oil in a wok or small pan and add the shallots and garlic. Stir-fry until golden, then remove from the heat and leave to cool. Put the minced pork into a bowl, add the stir-fried shallots and garlic, and add the *tuk trey*, five-spice powder and sugar. Season with a little salt and plenty of pepper. Using your hand, knead the mixture until well combined. Cover the bowl and chill in the refrigerator for 2–3 hours to allow the flavours to mingle. You can make this mixture a day ahead and leave it to marinate in the refrigerator overnight.

3 Soak eight wooden skewers in water for 30 minutes. Meanwhile, knead the mixture again, then add the breadcrumbs or potato starch. Knead well to bind. Divide the mixture into 20 pieces and roll into balls. Thread the balls on to the skewers. Cook either over the barbecue or under the grill (broiler), turning the skewers from time to time, until well browned.

4 Reheat the sauce, stirring constantly, and pour into a serving bowl. Arrange the meatballs on a serving dish with coriander leaves to wrap around them, or chop the coriander and use as a garnish. Serve with the sauce.

Per portion Energy 291Kcal/1216kJ; Protein 28g; Carbohydrate 15g, of which sugars 8g; Fat 14g, of which saturates 3g; Cholesterol 71mg; Calcium 69mg; Fibre 1.3g; Sodium 700mg

PORK AND BUTTERNUT CURRY

THIS CURRY CAN BE MADE WITH BUTTERNUT SQUASH, PUMPKIN OR WINTER MELON. FLAVOURED WITH KROEUNG, GALANGAL AND TURMERIC, IT IS DELICIOUS SERVED WITH RICE AND A FRUIT-BASED SALAD, OR EVEN JUST WITH CHUNKS OF FRESH CRUSTY BREAD TO MOP UP THE TASTY SAUCE.

SERVES FOUR TO SIX

INGREDIENTS

  30ml/2 tbsp groundnut (peanut) oil
  25g/1oz galangal, finely sliced
  2 red Thai chillies, peeled, seeded
    and finely sliced
  3 shallots, halved and finely sliced
  30ml/2 tbsp *kroeung*
  10ml/2 tsp ground turmeric
  5ml/1 tsp ground fenugreek
  10ml/2 tsp palm sugar
  450g/1lb pork loin, cut into
    bitesize chunks
  30ml/2 tbsp *tuk prahoc*
  900ml/1½ pints/3¾ cups
    coconut milk
  1 butternut squash, peeled, seeded
    and cut into bitesize chunks
  4 kaffir lime leaves
  sea salt and ground black pepper
  1 small bunch fresh coriander
    (cilantro), coarsely chopped and
    1 small bunch fresh mint, stalks
    removed, to garnish
  rice or noodles and salad, to serve

1 Heat the oil in a large wok or heavy pan. Stir in the galangal, chillies and shallots and stir-fry until fragrant. Add the *kroeung* and stir-fry until it begins to colour. Add the turmeric, fenugreek and sugar.

VARIATION
For a vegetarian option, omit the pork and use baby aubergines (eggplants) instead. The Cambodian flavourings and creamy coconut milk work well with many combinations.

2 Stir in the chunks of pork loin and stir-fry until golden brown on all sides. Stir in the *tuk prahoc* and pour in the coconut milk.

COOK'S TIP
Increase the number of chillies if you want a really hot curry.

3 Bring to the boil, add the squash and the lime leaves, and reduce the heat. Cook gently, uncovered, for 15–20 minutes, until the squash and pork are tender and the sauce has reduced. Season to taste. Garnish the curry with the coriander and mint, and serve with rice or noodles and salad.

Per portion Energy 188Kcal/789kJ; Protein 18g; Carbohydrate 13.2g, of which sugars 12.2g; Fat 7g, of which saturates 2g; Cholesterol 47mg; Calcium 97mg; Fibre 1.7g; Sodium 220mg

STEWED CARAMELIZED PIG'S FEET

THE KHMER, VIETNAMESE AND CHINESE COOK EVERY PART OF THE PIG — THE FEET, HOCKS AND SHANKS ARE STEWED SLOWLY. BECAUSE THE COOKING JUICES ARE SO RICH AND VELVETY FROM THE GELATINOUS MEAT, THIS DISH IS BEST SERVED WITH CHUNKS OF BREAD TO MOP UP THE SAUCE.

SERVES FOUR

INGREDIENTS

- 30ml/2 tbsp sugar
- 1 litre/1¾ pints/4 cups pork stock or water
- 30ml/2 tbsp *tuk trey*
- 30ml/2 tbsp soy sauce
- 900g/2lb pig's feet, cleaned
- 4 spring onions (scallions), trimmed, halved and bruised
- 2 lemon grass stalks, trimmed, halved and bruised
- 50g/2oz fresh root ginger, peeled and sliced
- 2 garlic cloves, crushed
- 2 dried red chillies
- 4 star anise
- 4 eggs, hard-boiled and shelled
- crusty bread or jasmine rice and stir-fried greens, to serve

2 Add the pig's feet, spring onions, lemon grass, ginger, garlic, chillies and star anise. Bring to the boil, then reduce the heat and cover the pan. Simmer for 3–4 hours, until the meat is very tender.

3 Skim any fat off the top and drop in the boiled eggs. Simmer uncovered for a further 10 minutes, turning the eggs over from time to time, so that they turn golden. Serve hot with fresh bread or jasmine rice and stir-fried greens.

1 In a heavy pan, melt the sugar with 15ml/1 tbsp water. When it turns golden, remove from the heat and stir in the stock or *tuk trey* and the soy sauce. Put the pan back over the heat and stir until the caramel dissolves.

Per portion Energy 126Kcal/531kJ; Protein 16g; Carbohydrate 8.6g, of which sugars 8.5g; Fat 3g, of which saturates 1g; Cholesterol 47mg; Calcium 19mg; Fibre 0.3g; Sodium 328mg

BAKED CINNAMON MEAT LOAF

SIMILAR TO THE VIETNAMESE STEAMED PÂTÉS, THIS TYPE OF MEAT LOAF IS USUALLY SERVED AS A SNACK OR LIGHT LUNCH, WITH A CRUSTY BAGUETTE. ACCOMPANIED WITH EITHER TART PICKLES OR A CRUNCHY SALAD, AND SPLASHED WITH PIQUANT SAUCE, IT IS LIGHT AND TASTY.

SERVES FOUR TO SIX

INGREDIENTS
  30ml/2 tbsp *tuk trey*
  25ml/1½ tbsp ground cinnamon
  10ml/2 tsp sugar
  5ml/1 tsp ground black pepper
  15ml/1 tbsp potato starch
  450g/1lb lean minced (ground) pork
  25g/1oz pork fat, very finely chopped
  2–3 shallots, very finely chopped
  oil, for greasing
  chilli oil or *tuk trey*, for drizzling
  red chilli strips, to garnish
  bread or noodles, to serve

2 Add the minced pork, the chopped pork fat, and the shallots to the bowl and mix thoroughly. Cover and put in the refrigerator for 3–4 hours.

4 Cover with foil and bake in the oven for 35–40 minutes. If you want the top to turn brown and crunchy, remove the foil for the last 10 minutes.

1 In a large bowl, mix together the *tuk trey*, ground cinnamon, sugar and ground black pepper. Beat in the potato starch.

3 Preheat the oven to 180°C/350°F/ Gas 4. Lightly oil a baking tin (pan) and spread the pork mixture in it – it should feel springy from the potato starch.

5 Turn the meat loaf out on to a board and slice it into strips. Drizzle the strips with chilli oil or *tuk trey*, and serve them hot with bread or noodles.

COOK'S TIPS
• Serve the meat loaf as a nibble with drinks by cutting it into bitesize squares or fingers.
• Serve with a piquant sauce for dipping.
• Cut the meat loaf into wedges and take on a picnic to eat with bread and pickles or chutney.
• Fry slices of meat loaf until browned and serve with fried eggs.

Per portion Energy 111Kcal/465kJ; Protein 16g; Carbohydrate 4.8g, of which sugars 2.3g; Fat 3g, of which saturates 1g; Cholesterol 47mg; Calcium 9mg; Fibre 0.2g; Sodium 54mg

CHICKEN <u>WITH</u> YOUNG GINGER

GINGER PLAYS A BIG ROLE IN CAMBODIAN COOKING, PARTICULARLY IN THE STIR-FRIED DISHES. WHENEVER POSSIBLE, THE JUICIER AND MORE PUNGENT YOUNG GINGER IS USED. THIS IS A SIMPLE AND DELICIOUS WAY TO COOK CHICKEN, PORK OR BEEF.

SERVES FOUR

INGREDIENTS
30ml/2 tbsp groundnut (peanut) oil
3 garlic cloves, finely sliced
  in strips
50g/2oz fresh young root ginger,
  finely sliced in strips
2 Thai chillies, seeded and finely
  sliced in strips
4 chicken breast fillets or 4 boned
  chicken legs, skinned and cut
  into bitesize chunks
30ml/2 tbsp *tuk prahoc*
10ml/2 tsp sugar
1 small bunch coriander (cilantro)
  stalks removed, roughly chopped
ground black pepper
jasmine rice and crunchy salad or
  baguette, to serve

1 Heat a wok or heavy pan and add the oil. Add the garlic, ginger and chillies, and stir-fry until fragrant and golden. Add the chicken and toss it around the wok for 1–2 minutes.

COOK'S TIP
Young ginger is available in Chinese and South-east Asian markets.

2 Stir in the *tuk prahoc* and sugar, and stir-fry for a further 4–5 minutes until cooked. Season with pepper and add some of the fresh coriander. Transfer the chicken to a serving dish and garnish with the remaining coriander. Serve hot with jasmine rice and a crunchy salad with fresh herbs, or with chunks of freshly baked baguette.

Per portion Energy 222Kcal/935kJ; Protein 36.4g; Carbohydrate 3g, of which sugars 2.9g; Fat 7.3g, of which saturates 1.1g; Cholesterol 105mg; Calcium 32mg; Fibre 0.6g; Sodium 100mg

CHICKEN AND VEGETABLE STEW

SAMLAA KAKO IS ONE OF THE MOST POPULAR CAMBODIAN DISHES ON RESTAURANT MENUS AND IT IS COOKED DAILY IN PEOPLE'S HOMES. THERE ARE MANY DIFFERENT VERSIONS, DEPENDING ON THE AREA AND WHICH VEGETABLES ARE IN SEASON, BUT IT IS ALWAYS DELICIOUS.

SERVES FOUR TO SIX

INGREDIENTS

   30ml/2 tbsp groundnut (peanut) oil
   4 garlic cloves, halved and crushed
   25g/1oz galangal, peeled and
     finely sliced
   2 chillies
   30ml/2 tbsp *kroeung*
   15ml/1 tbsp palm sugar
   12 chicken thighs
   30ml/2 tbsp *tuk prahoc*
   a handful kaffir lime leaves
   600ml/1 pint/2½ cups coconut milk
   350g/12oz pumpkin flesh, seeded
     and cut into bitesize chunks
   1 long Asian or Mediterranean
     aubergine (eggplant), quartered
     lengthways, each quarter cut into 3
   115g/4oz long beans, trimmed and
     cut into 5cm/2in lengths
   3 tomatoes, skinned, quartered,
     and seeded
   a handful morning glory or spinach
     leaves, washed and trimmed
   a small bunch basil leaves
   sea salt and ground black pepper
   1 small bunch each fresh coriander
     (cilantro) and mint, stalks removed,
     coarsely chopped, to garnish
   jasmine rice, to serve

COOK'S TIP
A meal in itself, a big pot of *samlaa kako* is placed in the middle of the table and everyone helps themselves. Sometimes it includes rice cooked in it, at other times it is served with jasmine rice.

1 Heat the groundnut oil in a wok or heavy pan. Add the garlic, galangal and whole chillies and stir-fry until fragrant and golden. Stir in the *kroeung* and sugar, until it has dissolved. Add the chicken, tossing it well, and stir in the *tuk prahoc*, kaffir lime leaves and coconut milk. Reduce the heat and simmer for 10 minutes.

2 Add the pumpkin, aubergine and snake beans and simmer until tender. If you need to add more liquid, stir in a little water. Add the tomatoes and morning glory or spinach, and the basil leaves. Cook for a further 2 minutes, then season to taste with salt and pepper. Garnish with coriander and mint and serve hot with jasmine rice.

Per portion Energy 418Kcal/1747kJ; Protein 31g; Carbohydrate 15g, of which sugars 14.3g; Fat 26.4g, of which saturates 6.7g; Cholesterol 160mg; Calcium 127mg; Fibre 3g; Sodium 350mg

CARAMELIZED CHICKEN WINGS WITH GINGER

COOKED IN A WOK OR IN THE OVEN, THESE CARAMELIZED WINGS ARE DRIZZLED WITH CHILLI OIL AND EATEN WITH THE FINGERS, AND EVERY BIT OF TENDER MEAT IS SUCKED OFF THE BONE. OFTEN SERVED WITH RICE AND PICKLES, VARIATIONS OF THIS RECIPE CAN BE FOUND IN VIETNAM AND CAMBODIA.

SERVES TWO TO FOUR

INGREDIENTS
　75ml/5 tbsp sugar
　30ml/2 tbsp groundnut (peanut) oil
　25g/1oz fresh root ginger, peeled and
　　finely shredded or grated
　12 chicken wings, split in two
　chilli oil, for drizzling
　mixed pickled vegetables,
　　to serve

1 To make a caramel sauce, gently heat the sugar with 60ml/4 tbsp water in a small, heavy pan until it turns golden, Set aside.

2 Heat the oil in a wok or heavy pan. Add the ginger and stir-fry until fragrant. Add the chicken wings and toss them around the wok to brown.

3 Pour in the caramel sauce and make sure the chicken wings are coated in it. Reduce the heat, cover the wok or pan, and cook for about 30 minutes, until tender, and the sauce has caramelized.

4 Drizzle chilli oil over the wings and serve from the wok or pan with mixed pickled vegetables.

Per portion Energy 393Kcal/1641kJ; Protein 30.5g; Carbohydrate 14.4g, of which sugars 14.4g; Fat 24g, of which saturates 6.3g; Cholesterol 134mg; Calcium 16mg; Fibre 0g; Sodium 100mg

STIR-FRIED FROG'S LEGS

Frog's legs are popular throughout South-east Asia. Sold live in the markets, plump frogs are beheaded, skinned and cleaned for keen cooks, as the whole frog is edible. This is one of the most delicious ways of cooking frog's legs with richly fragrant KROEUNG.

SERVES THREE TO FOUR

INGREDIENTS

    15ml/1 tbsp groundnut
      (peanut) oil
    2 garlic cloves, finely chopped
    2 Thai chillies, seeded and
      finely chopped
    30ml/2 tbsp *kroeung*
    15ml/1 tbsp *tuk prahoc*
    15ml/1 tbsp palm sugar
    4 fresh kaffir lime leaves
    6 pairs of frog's legs, separated
      into 12 single legs, rinsed and
      dabbed dry
    chilli oil, for drizzling

VARIATION
You can garnish the frog's legs with
chopped fresh herbs, such as coriander
(cilantro) or basil, if you like.

1 Heat the oil in a wok or heavy pan.
Stir in the garlic and chillies, until they
become fragrant. Add the *kroeung, tuk
prahoc* and sugar and stir-fry until it
begins to colour. Add the lime leaves
and frog's legs, tossing them around the
wok to make sure they are coated in the
sauce. Arrange the legs against the
base and sides of the wok to fry on both
sides, until brown and crisp.

2 Transfer the frog's legs to a warmed
serving dish and drizzle with chilli oil.
Serve with garlic and ginger rice and
a salad.

COOK'S TIP
Frog's legs, often sold in pairs, can be
bought fresh and frozen in Asian markets.
They are prized for stir-fries, where they
are cooked with garlic and herbs.

Per portion Energy 113Kcal/475kJ; Protein 12.4g; Carbohydrate 8.5g, of which sugars 8.2g; Fat 3.4g, of which saturates 0.5g; Cholesterol 35mg; Calcium 22mg; Fibre 0.5g; Sodium 480mg

RICE & NOODLES

Rice, noodles, or a combination of both, form the foundation of every Cambodian meal. Rice can either be the standard aromatic variety or the glutinous type; the latter is soaked before being steamed and is often used in desserts. Rice Porridge or Garlic and Ginger Rice with Coriander are both popular for breakfast, and all rice and noodle dishes are eaten throughout the day as snacks — for instance Coconut Rice or Wheat Noodles with Stir-fried Pork.

STEAMED RICE

LONG AND SHORT GRAIN RICE IS GENERALLY STEAMED OR BOILED AND SERVED AT MOST MEALS, OR IT IS SUBSTITUTED WITH BREAD, A LEGACY OF THE FRENCH. IN CAMBODIAN VILLAGES, RICE IS OFTEN STEAMED IN THE HOLLOW OF A BAMBOO STEM, A VESSEL THAT LENDS A UNIQUE FLAVOUR TO THE RICE.

SERVES FOUR

INGREDIENTS
   225g/8oz/generous 1 cup long grain
     rice, rinsed and drained
   a pinch of salt

1 Put the rice into a heavy pan or clay pot. Add 600ml/1 pint/2½ cups water to cover the rice by 2.5cm/1in. Add the salt, and then bring the water to the boil.

VARIATION
Jasmine rice is delicious and readily available from Asian stores.

2 Reduce the heat, cover the pan and cook gently for about 20 minutes, or until all the water has been absorbed. Remove the pan from the heat and leave to steam, still covered, for a further 5–10 minutes.

3 To serve, simply fluff up with a fork.

Per portion Energy 203Kcal/864kJ; Protein 4g; Carbohydrate 49g, of which sugars 0g; Fat 1g, of which saturates 0g; Cholesterol 0mg; Calcium 2mg; Fibre 0.3g; Sodium 0mg

BAMBOO-STEAMED STICKY RICE

STICKY, OR GLUTINOUS, RICE REQUIRES A LONG SOAK IN WATER BEFORE BEING COOKED IN A BAMBOO STEAMER. THROUGHOUT SOUTH-EAST ASIA IT IS USED FOR SAVOURY AND SWEET DISHES, SUCH AS STICKY RICE WITH DURIAN SAUCE. STICKY RICE IS AVAILABLE IN CHINESE AND ASIAN STORES.

SERVES FOUR

INGREDIENTS
350g/12oz/1¾ cups sticky rice

1 Put the rice into a large bowl and fill the bowl with cold water. Leave the rice to soak for at least 6 hours, then drain, rinse thoroughly, and drain again.

VARIATION
Sticky rice is enjoyed as a sweet, filling snack with sugar and coconut milk and, as it is fairly bulky, it is also served with dipping sauces, light dishes and vegetarian meals.

2 Fill a wok or heavy pan one-third full with water. Place a bamboo steamer, with the lid on, over the wok or pan and bring the water to the boil. Uncover the steamer and place a dampened piece of muslin (cheesecloth) over the rack. Tip the rice into the middle and spread it out. Fold the muslin over the rice, cover and steam for 25 minutes until the rice is tender but firm. The measured quantity of rice grains doubles when cooked.

Per portion Energy 314Kcal/1314kJ; Protein 7g; Carbohydrate 66g, of which sugars 0g; Fat 1g, of which saturates 0g; Cholesterol 0mg; Calcium 14mg; Fibre 0g; Sodium 0mg

SOUTHERN-SPICED CHILLI RICE

ALTHOUGH PLAIN STEAMED RICE IS SERVED AT ALMOST EVERY MEAL, MANY SOUTHERN FAMILIES LIKE TO SNEAK IN A LITTLE SPICE TOO. A BURST OF CHILLI FOR FIRE, TURMERIC FOR COLOUR, AND CORIANDER FOR ITS COOLING FLAVOUR, ARE ALL THAT'S NEEDED.

SERVES FOUR

INGREDIENTS
  15ml/1 tbsp vegetable oil
  2–3 green or red Thai chillies,
    seeded and finely chopped
  2 garlic cloves, finely chopped
  2.5cm/1in fresh root ginger, chopped
  5ml/1 tsp sugar
  10–15ml/2–3 tsp ground turmeric
  225g/8oz/generous 1 cup long
    grain rice
  30ml/2 tbsp *tuk trey*
  600ml/1 pint/2½ cups water or stock
  1 bunch of fresh coriander
    (cilantro), stalks removed, leaves
    finely chopped
  salt and ground black pepper

1 Heat the oil in a heavy pan. Stir in the chillies, garlic and ginger with the sugar. As they begin to colour, stir in the turmeric. Add the rice, coating it well, then pour in the *tuk trey* and the water or stock – the liquid should sit about 2.5cm/1in above the rice.

2 Tip the rice on to a serving dish. Add some of the coriander and lightly toss together using a fork. Garnish with the remaining coriander.

COOK'S TIP
This rice goes well with grilled and stir-fried fish and shellfish dishes, but you can serve it as an alternative to plain rice. Add extra chillies, if you like.

3 Season with salt and ground black pepper and bring the liquid to the boil. Reduce the heat, cover and simmer for about 25 minutes, or until the water has been absorbed. Remove from the heat and leave the rice to steam for a further 10 minutes.

RICE PORRIDGE

IN CAMBODIA, A STEAMING BOWL OF THICK RICE PORRIDGE OR BOBOR IS A NOURISHING AND SATISFYING BREAKFAST. USUALLY MADE WITH LONG GRAIN RICE, IT CAN BE MADE PLAIN, OR WITH THE ADDITION OF CHICKEN, PORK, FISH OR PRAWNS.

SERVES SIX

INGREDIENTS

- 15ml/1 tbsp vegetable or groundnut (peanut) oil
- 25g/1oz fresh root ginger, shredded
- 115g/4oz/generous 1 cup long grain rice, rinsed and drained
- 1.2 litres/2 pints/5 cups chicken stock or water
- 30–45ml/2–3 tbsp *tuk trey*
- 10ml/2 tsp sugar
- 450g/1lb fresh fish fillets, boned (any fish will do)
- sea salt and ground black pepper

For the garnish

- 15ml/1 tbsp vegetable or groundnut (peanut) oil
- 2 garlic cloves, finely chopped
- 1 lemon grass stalk, trimmed and finely sliced
- 25g/1oz fresh root ginger, shredded
- a few coriander (cilantro) leaves

1 In a heavy pan heat the oil and stir in the ginger and rice for 1 minute. Pour in the stock and bring it to the boil. Reduce the heat and simmer, partially covered, for 20 minutes, until the rice is tender and the soup is thick. Stir the *tuk trey* and sugar into the soupy porridge. Season and keep the porridge hot.

2 Meanwhile, fill a wok a third of the way with water. Fit a covered bamboo steamer on top and bring the water to the boil so that the steam rises. Season the fish fillets, place them on a plate and put them inside the steamer. Cover and steam the fish until cooked.

3 For the garnish, heat the oil in small wok or heavy pan. Add the chopped garlic, lemon grass and ginger and stir-fry until golden and fragrant. Add chillies to the mixture, if you like.

4 Ladle the rice porridge into bowls. Tear off pieces of steamed fish fillet to place on top. Sprinkle with the stir-fried garlic, lemon grass and ginger, and garnish with a few coriander leaves.

Per portion Energy 152Kcal/636kJ; Protein 15g; Carbohydrate 17g, of which sugars 1.7g; Fat 2g, of which saturates 0.3g; Cholesterol 35mg; Calcium 11mg; Fibre 0g; Sodium 45mg

GARLIC AND GINGER RICE WITH CORIANDER

IN CAMBODIA, STEAMED RICE IS GENERALLY SERVED PLAIN, OR ALTERNATIVELY WITH THE DISTINCT FLAVOURS OF GARLIC AND GINGER, WHICH COMPLEMENT MOST VEGETABLE, FISH OR MEAT DISHES. THIS PUNGENT RICE IS ALSO VERY POPULAR FOR BREAKFAST.

SERVES FOUR TO SIX

INGREDIENTS

- 15ml/1 tbsp vegetable or groundnut (peanut) oil
- 2–3 garlic cloves, finely chopped
- 25g/1oz fresh root ginger, finely chopped
- 225g/8oz/generous 1 cup long grain rice, rinsed in several bowls of water and drained
- 900ml/1½ pints/3¾ cups chicken stock
- a bunch of fresh coriander (cilantro) leaves, finely chopped
- a bunch of fresh basil and mint, (optional), finely chopped

1 Heat the oil in a clay pot or heavy pan. Stir in the garlic and ginger and fry until golden. Stir in the rice and allow it to absorb the flavours for 1–2 minutes. Pour in the stock and stir to make sure the rice doesn't stick. Bring the stock to the boil, then reduce the heat.

2 Scatter the coriander over the surface of the stock, cover the pan, and leave to cook gently for 20–25 minutes, until the rice has absorbed all the liquid. Turn off the heat and gently fluff up the rice to mix in the coriander. Cover and leave to infuse for 10 minutes before serving.

Per portion Energy 151Kcal/632kJ; Protein 3g; Carbohydrate 30g, of which sugars 0g; Fat 2g, of which saturates 0.3g; Cholesterol 0mg; Calcium 9mg; Fibre 0.1g; Sodium 124mg

COCONUT RICE

ORIGINALLY PREPARED IN INDIA AND THAILAND, COCONUT RICE IS POPULAR IN CAMBODIA. RICH AND NOURISHING, IT IS OFTEN SERVED WITH A TANGY FRUIT AND VEGETABLE SALAD, SUCH AS GREEN PAPAYA OR GREEN MANGO. THIS DISH COMBINES WELL WITH A HOT CURRY.

SERVES FOUR TO SIX

INGREDIENTS
 400ml/14fl oz/1⅔ cups unsweetened
  coconut milk
 400ml/14fl oz/1⅔ cups seasoned
  chicken stock
 225g/8oz/generous 1 cup long grain
  rice, rinsed in several bowls of
  water and drained
 115g/4oz fresh coconut, grated

COOK'S TIP
As the coconut shells are often halved and used as bowls, they make a perfect serving vessel for this rice, garnished with fresh or roasted coconut or crispy-fried ginger. In the street, this rice is often served on a banana leaf.

1 Pour the coconut milk and stock into a heavy pan and stir well to combine. Bring the liquid to the boil and stir in the rice. Stir once, reduce the heat and cover the pan. Simmer gently for about 25 minutes, until the rice has absorbed all the liquid. Remove from the heat and leave the rice to sit for 10 minutes.

2 Meanwhile, heat a small, heavy pan. Stir in the fresh coconut and roast it until it turns golden with a nutty aroma. Tip the roasted coconut into a bowl.

3 Fluff up the rice with a fork and spoon it into bowls. Scatter the roasted coconut over the top and serve.

Per portion Energy 175Kcal/731kJ; Protein 3g; Carbohydrate 33.5g, of which sugars 3.5g; Fat 3g, of which saturates 2g; Cholesterol 0mg; Calcium 28mg; Fibre 0.6g; Sodium 75mg

FRESH RICE NOODLES

A VARIETY OF DRIED NOODLES IS AVAILABLE IN ASIAN SUPERMARKETS, BUT FRESH ONES ARE QUITE DIFFERENT AND NOT THAT DIFFICULT TO MAKE. THE FRESHLY MADE NOODLE SHEETS CAN BE SERVED AS A SNACK, DRENCHED IN SUGAR OR HONEY, OR DIPPED INTO A SAVOURY SAUCE OF YOUR CHOICE.

SERVES FOUR

INGREDIENTS

   225g/8oz/2 cups rice flour
   600ml/1 pint/2½ cups water
   a pinch of salt
   15ml/1 tbsp vegetable oil, plus extra
     for brushing
   slivers of red chilli and fresh root
     ginger, and coriander (cilantro)
     leaves, to garnish (optional)

1 Place the flour in a bowl and stir in some of the water to form a paste. Pour in the rest of the water, beating it to make a lump-free batter. Add the salt and oil and leave to stand for 15 minutes.

COOK'S TIP

You may need to top up the water through one of the slits and tighten the cloth.

2 Meanwhile, fill a wide pan with water. Cut a piece of smooth cotton cloth a little larger than the diameter of the pan. Stretch it over the top of the pan, pulling the edges tautly down over the sides, then wind a piece of string around the edge, to secure. Using a sharp knife, make three small slits, about 2.5cm/1in from the edge of the cloth, at regular intervals.

3 Bring the water to the boil. Stir the batter and ladle 30–45ml/2–3 tbsp on to the cloth, swirling it to form a 13–15cm/5–6in wide circle. Cover with a domed lid, such as a wok lid, and steam for 1 minute, or until the noodle sheet is translucent.

4 Carefully insert a spatula or knife under the noodle sheet and prise it off the cloth. (If it doesn't peel off easily, you may need to steam it a little longer.) Transfer the noodle sheet to a lightly oiled baking tray, brush lightly with oil, and cook the remaining batter in the same way.

VARIATION

Fresh noodles can be cut into strips and stir-fried with garlic, ginger, chillies and *tuk trey* dipping sauce or soy sauce.

Per portion Energy 251Kcal/1046kJ; Protein 4g; Carbohydrate 45g, of which sugars 0g; Fat 5g, of which saturates 1g; Cholesterol 0mg; Calcium 24mg; Fibre 1.1g; Sodium 200mg

WHEAT NOODLES WITH STIR-FRIED PORK

WHEAT NOODLES ARE POPULAR IN CAMBODIA. SOLD DRIED, IN STRAIGHT BUNDLES LIKE STICKS, THEY ARE VERSATILE AND ROBUST. NOODLES DRYING IN THE OPEN AIR, HANGING FROM BAMBOO POLES, ARE COMMON IN THE MARKETS. THIS SIMPLE RECIPE COMES FROM A NOODLE STALL IN PHNOM PENH.

SERVES FOUR

INGREDIENTS

- 225g/8oz pork loin, cut into thin strips
- 225g/8oz dried wheat noodles, soaked in lukewarm water for 20 minutes
- 15ml/1 tbsp groundnut (peanut) oil
- 2 garlic cloves, finely chopped
- 2–3 spring onions (scallions), trimmed and cut into bitesize pieces
- 45ml/3 tbsp *kroeung*
- 15ml/1 tbsp *tuk trey*
- 30ml/2 tbsp unsalted roasted peanuts, finely chopped
- chilli oil, for drizzling

For the marinade
- 30ml/2 tbsp *tuk trey*
- 30ml/2 tbsp soy sauce
- 15ml/1 tbsp peanut oil
- 10ml/2 tsp sugar

1 In a bowl, combine the ingredients for the marinade, stirring constantly until the all the sugar dissolves. Toss in the strips of pork, making sure they are well coated in the marinade. Then put aside for 30 minutes.

2 Drain the wheat noodles. Bring a large pan of water to the boil. Drop in the noodles, untangling them with chopsticks, if necessary. Cook for 4–5 minutes, until tender. Allow the noodles to drain thoroughly, then divide them among individual serving bowls. Keep the noodles warm until the dish is ready to serve.

3 Meanwhile, heat a wok. Add the oil and stir-fry the garlic and spring onions, until fragrant. Add the pork, tossing it around the wok for 2 minutes. Stir in the *kroeung* and *tuk trey* for 2 minutes – add a splash of water if the wok gets too dry – and tip the pork on top of the noodles. Sprinkle the peanuts over the top and drizzle with chilli oil to serve.

Per portion Energy 357Kcal/1494kJ; Protein 17g; Carbohydrate 51g, of which sugars 4.8g; Fat 9g, of which saturates 2g; Cholesterol 35mg; Calcium 21mg; Fibre 0.7g; Sodium 495mg

VEGETABLES, SALADS & SAUCES

Raw, stir-fried, braised, pickled or salted, vegetables appear frequently on the Cambodian table. For a tasty warm meal, try Glazed Pumpkin in Coconut Milk, or Vegetarian Stir-fry with Peanut Sauce, prepare Pickled Ginger for use in a soup, or use fruit such as mango or banana in a refreshing salad. Dips, sauces and condiments are present at every meal — with favourites being the fish extract tuk prahoc *and* tuk trey, *a fish sauce with roasted peanuts.*

AUBERGINE CURRY <u>WITH</u> COCONUT MILK

AUBERGINE CURRIES ARE POPULAR THROUGHOUT SOUTH-EAST ASIA, THE THAI VERSION BEING THE MOST FAMOUS. ALL ARE HOT AND AROMATIC, ENRICHED WITH COCONUT MILK. THIS KHMER RECIPE USES THE TRADEMARK HERBAL PASTE, KROEUNG.

2 Stir in the coconut milk and stock, and add the aubergines and lime leaves.

3 Partially cover the pan and simmer over a gentle heat for about 25 minutes until the aubergines are tender. Stir in the basil and check the seasoning. Serve with jasmine rice and lime wedges.

SERVES FOUR TO SIX

INGREDIENTS
    15ml/1 tbsp vegetable oil
    4 garlic cloves, crushed
    2 shallots, sliced
    2 dried chillies
    45ml/3 tbsp *kroeung*
    15ml/1 tbsp shrimp paste or *tuk prahoc*
    15ml/1 tbsp palm sugar
    600ml/1 pint/2½ cups coconut milk
    250ml/8fl oz/1 cup chicken stock
    4 aubergines (eggplants), trimmed
        and cut into bitesize pieces
    6 kaffir lime leaves
    1 bunch fresh basil, stalks removed
    jasmine rice and 2 limes, cut into
        quarters, to serve
    salt and ground black pepper

1 Heat the oil in a wok or heavy pan. Stir in the garlic, shallots and whole chillies and stir-fry until they begin to colour. Stir in the *kroeung*, shrimp paste or *tuk prahoc* and palm sugar and stir-fry until the mixture begins to darken.

Per portion Energy 72Kcal/305kJ; Protein 1.6g; Carbohydrate 11.2g, of which sugars 10.7g; Fat 3g, of which saturates 1g; Cholesterol 0mg; Calcium 46mg; Fibre 2.8g; Sodium 113mg

STIR-FRIED PINEAPPLE WITH GINGER

THROUGHOUT SOUTH-EAST ASIA, FRUIT IS OFTEN TREATED LIKE A VEGETABLE AND TOSSED IN A SALAD, OR STIR-FRIED, TO ACCOMPANY SPICY DISHES. IN THIS DISH, THE PINEAPPLE IS COMBINED WITH THE TANGY FLAVOURS OF GINGER AND CHILLI AND SERVED AS A SIDE DISH.

SERVES FOUR

INGREDIENTS
30ml/2 tbsp groundnut (peanut) oil
2 garlic cloves, finely shredded
40g/1½oz fresh root ginger, peeled and finely shredded
2 red Thai chillies, seeded and finely shredded
1 pineapple, trimmed, peeled, cored and cut into bitesize chunks
15ml/1 tbsp *tuk trey*
30ml/2 tbsp soy sauce
15ml–30ml/1–2 tbsp sugar
30ml/2 tbsp roasted unsalted peanuts, finely chopped
1 lime, cut into quarters, to serve

1 Heat a large wok or heavy pan and add the oil. Stir in the garlic, ginger and chilli. Stir-fry until they begin to colour, then add the pineapple and stir-fry for a further 1–2 minutes, until the edges turn golden.

2 Add the *tuk trey*, soy sauce and sugar to taste and continue to stir-fry until the pineapple begins to caramelize.

3 Transfer to a serving dish, sprinkle with the roasted peanuts and serve with lime wedges.

Per portion Energy 185Kcal/780kJ; Protein 3g; Carbohydrate 24.1g, of which sugars 23.6g; Fat 9g, of which saturates 1g; Cholesterol 0mg; Calcium 43mg; Fibre 2.9g; Sodium 271mg

VEGETARIAN STIR-FRY WITH PEANUT SAUCE

STIR-FRIED VEGETABLES ARE POPULAR THROUGHOUT SOUTH-EAST ASIA. WHEREVER YOU GO, THERE WILL BE SOME VARIATION ON THE THEME. IN CAMBODIA, THE VEGETABLES ARE SOMETIMES DRIZZLED IN A PEANUT SAUCE LIKE THIS ONE, PARTICULARLY AMONG THE BUDDHIST COMMUNITIES.

SERVES FOUR TO SIX

INGREDIENTS

   6 Chinese black mushrooms (dried shiitake), soaked in lukewarm water for 20 minutes
   20 tiger lily buds, soaked in lukewarm water for 20 minutes
   225g/8oz tofu
   60ml/4 tbsp sesame or groundnut (peanut) oil
   1 large onion, halved and finely sliced
   1 large carrot, finely sliced
   300g/11oz pak choi (bok choy), the leaves separated from the stems
   225g/8oz can bamboo shoots, drained and rinsed
   50ml/2fl oz/¼ cup soy sauce
   10ml/2 tsp sugar
For the peanut sauce
   15ml/1 tbsp groundnut (peanut) or sesame oil
   2 garlic cloves, finely chopped
   2 red chillies, seeded and finely chopped
   90g/3½oz/generous ½ cup unsalted roasted peanuts, finely chopped
   150ml/5fl oz/⅔ cup coconut milk
   30ml/2 tbsp hoisin sauce
   15ml/1 tbsp soy sauce
   15ml/1 tbsp sugar

1 To make the sauce, heat the oil in a small wok or heavy pan. Stir in the garlic and chillies, stir-fry until they begin to colour, then add all the peanuts except 15ml/1 tbsp. Stir-fry for a few minutes until the natural oil from the peanuts begins to weep.

VARIATION

The popular piquant peanut sauce is delicious served hot with stir-fried, deep-fried or steamed vegetables. Alternatively, leave it to cool, garnish with a little chopped mint and coriander (cilantro) and serve it as a dip for raw vegetables, such as strips of carrot, cucumber and celery.

2 Add the remaining ingredients and bring to the boil. Reduce the heat and cook gently until the sauce thickens a little and specks of oil appear on the surface. Put aside.

3 Drain the mushrooms and lily buds and squeeze out any excess water. Cut the mushroom caps into strips and discard the stalks. Trim off the hard ends of the lily buds and tie a knot in the centre of each one. Put the mushrooms and lily buds aside.

4 Cut the tofu into slices. Heat 30ml/2 tbsp of the oil in a wok or heavy pan and brown the tofu on both sides. Drain on kitchen paper and cut it into strips.

5 Heat a wok or heavy pan and add the remaining oil. Stir in the onion and carrot and stir-fry for a minute. Add the pak choi stems and stir-fry for 2 minutes. Add the mushrooms, lily buds, tofu and bamboo shoots and stir-fry for a minute more. Toss in the pak choi leaves, followed by the soy sauce and sugar. Stir-fry until heated through.

6 Heat up the peanut sauce and drizzle over the vegetables in the wok, or spoon the vegetables into individual bowls and top with a little sauce. Garnish with the remaining peanuts and serve.

Per portion Energy 252Kcal/1045kJ; Protein 10g; Carbohydrate 12g, of which sugars 8.5g; Fat 18g, of which saturates 3g; Cholesterol 0mg; Calcium 319mg; Fibre 3.6g; Sodium 1055mg

STIR-FRIED LONG BEANS WITH PRAWNS

LONG BEANS ARE A POPULAR INGREDIENT OF THE REGION AND — LIKE MANY OTHER VEGETABLES — THEY ARE OFTEN STIR-FRIED WITH GARLIC. THIS RECIPE IS LIVENED UP WITH PRAWNS, AS WELL AS OTHER FLAVOURINGS, AND WORKS WELL EITHER AS A SIDE DISH OR ON ITS OWN WITH RICE.

3 Heat 30ml/2 tbsp of the oil in a wok. Stir in the chopped garlic and galangal. As they begin to colour, toss in the marinated prawns. Stir-fry for a minute or until the prawns turn pink. Lift the prawns out, reserving as much of the oil, garlic and galangal as you can.

4 Add the remaining oil to the wok. Add the onion and stir-fry until slightly caramelized. Stir in the beans, then pour in the soy sauce. Cook for a further 2–3 minutes, until the beans are tender. Add the prawns and stir-fry for a minute until heated through. Serve immediately.

SERVES FOUR

INGREDIENTS
    45ml/3 tbsp vegetable oil
    2 garlic cloves, finely chopped
    25g/1oz galangal, finely shredded
    450g/1lb fresh prawns (shrimp),
      shelled and deveined
    1 onion, halved and finely sliced
    450g/1lb long beans, trimmed and
      cut into 7.5cm/3in lengths
    120ml/4fl oz/½ cup soy sauce
For the marinade
    30ml/2 tbsp *tuk trey*
    juice of 2 limes
    10ml/2 tsp sugar
    2 garlic cloves, crushed
    1 lemon grass stalk, trimmed and
      finely sliced

1 To make the marinade, beat the *tuk trey* and the lime juice in a bowl with the sugar, until it has dissolved. Then stir in the garlic and lemon grass.

2 Toss in the prawns, cover the bowl, and chill for 1–2 hours.

Per portion Energy 215Kcal/897kJ; Protein 23g; Carbohydrate 10g, of which sugars 8.2g; Fat 9g, of which saturates 1g; Cholesterol 219mg; Calcium 140mg; Fibre 2.7g; Sodium 235mg

GLAZED PUMPKIN IN COCONUT MILK

PUMPKINS, BUTTERNUT SQUASH AND WINTER MELONS CAN ALL BE COOKED IN THIS WAY. THROUGHOUT CAMBODIA AND VIETNAM, VARIATIONS OF THIS SWEET, MELLOW DISH ARE OFTEN SERVED AS AN ACCOMPANIMENT TO RICE OR A SPICY CURRY.

SERVES FOUR

INGREDIENTS

200ml/7fl oz/scant 1 cup
  coconut milk
15ml/1 tbsp *tuk trey*
30ml/2 tbsp palm sugar
30ml/2 tbsp groundnut (peanut) oil
4 garlic cloves, finely chopped
25g/1oz fresh root ginger, peeled and
  finely shredded
675g/1½lb pumpkin flesh, cubed
ground black pepper
a handful of curry or basil leaves,
  to garnish
chilli oil, for drizzling
fried onion rings, to garnish
plain or coconut rice, to serve

1 In a bowl, beat the coconut milk and the *tuk trey* with the sugar, until it has dissolved. Set aside.

2 Heat the oil in a wok or heavy pan and stir in the garlic and ginger. Stir-fry until they begin to colour, then stir in the pumpkin cubes, mixing well.

3 Pour in the coconut milk and mix well. Reduce the heat, cover and simmer for about 20 minutes, until the pumpkin is tender and the sauce has reduced. Season with pepper and garnish with curry or basil leaves and fried onion rings. Serve hot with plain or coconut rice, drizzled with a little chilli oil.

Per portion Energy 114Kcal/477kJ; Protein 1.5g; Carbohydrate 14g, of which sugars 13.4g; Fat 6g, of which saturates 1g; Cholesterol 0mg; Calcium 68mg; Fibre 1.7g; Sodium 323mg

PICKLED VEGETABLES

EVERYDAY CAMBODIAN PICKLES GENERALLY CONSIST OF CUCUMBER, MOOLI AND CARROT — GREEN, WHITE AND ORANGE IN COLOUR — AND ARE SERVED FOR NIBBLING ON, AS PART OF THE TABLE SALAD, OR AS AN ACCOMPANIMENT TO GRILLED MEATS AND SHELLFISH.

SERVES FOUR TO SIX

INGREDIENTS
- 300ml/½ pint/1¼ cups white rice vinegar
- 90g/3½oz/½ cup sugar
- 450g/1lb carrots, cut into 5cm/2in matchsticks
- 450g/1lb mooli (daikon), halved lengthways, and cut into thin crescents
- 600g/1lb 6oz cucumber, partially peeled in strips and cut into 5cm/2in matchsticks
- 15ml/1 tbsp salt

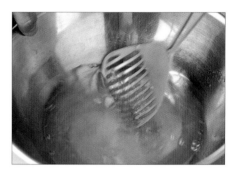

1 In a large bowl, whisk the vinegar with the sugar, until it dissolves.

2 Add the carrots and daikon to the vinegar mixture and toss well to coat. Cover them and place in the refrigerator for 24 hours, turning them occasionally.

3 Put the cucumber on a plate and sprinkle with the salt. Leave for 30 minutes, then rinse under cold water and drain well. Add to the carrot and daikon and toss well in the pickling liquid. Cover and refrigerate as before.

4 Lift the vegetables out of the pickling liquid to serve, or spoon them into a jar and store in the refrigerator.

Per portion Energy 104Kcal/438kJ; Protein 2g; Carbohydrate 24g, of which sugars 24g; Fat 0.5g, of which saturates 0.2g; Cholesterol 0mg; Calcium 59mg; Fibre 3.1g; Sodium 1013mg

PICKLED GINGER

THE CAMBODIANS LOVE COOKING WITH GINGER. WARMING, GOOD FOR THE HEART, AND BELIEVED TO AID DIGESTION, IT FINDS ITS WAY INTO SALADS, SOUPS, STIR-FRIES AND PUDDINGS. CHINESE IN ORIGIN, PICKLED GINGER IS OFTEN SERVED AS A CONDIMENT WITH BROTHS, NOODLES AND RICE.

SERVES FOUR TO SIX

INGREDIENTS
   225g/8oz fresh young ginger, peeled
   10ml/2 tsp salt
   200ml/7fl oz/1 cup white rice vinegar
   50g/2oz/¼ cup sugar

1 Place the ginger in a bowl and sprinkle with salt. Cover and place in the refrigerator for 24 hours.

COOK'S TIP
Juicy and tender with a pinkish-yellow skin, young ginger is less fibrous than the mature rhizome. When pickled in vinegar, the flesh turns pale pink.

2 Drain off any liquid and pat the ginger dry with a clean dishtowel. Slice each knob of ginger very finely along the grain, like thin rose petals, and place them in a clean bowl or a sterilized jar suitable for storing.

3 In a small bowl beat the vinegar and 50ml/2fl oz/¼ cup water with the sugar, until it has dissolved. Pour the pickling liquid over the ginger and cover or seal. Store in the refrigerator or a cool place for about a week.

Per portion Energy 36Kcal/151kJ; Protein 0.2g; Carbohydrate 9.1g, of which sugars 9.1g; Fat 0.1g, of which saturates 0g; Cholesterol 0mg; Calcium 20mg; Fibre 0.4g; Sodium 678mg

GREEN MANGO SALAD

ALTHOUGH THE ORANGE AND YELLOW MANGOES AND PAPAYAS ARE DEVOURED IN VAST QUANTITIES WHEN RIPE AND JUICY, THEY ARE ALSO POPULAR WHEN GREEN. THEIR TART FLAVOUR AND CRUNCHY TEXTURE MAKE THEM IDEAL FOR SALADS AND STEWS.

SERVES FOUR

INGREDIENTS

   450g/1lb green mangoes
   grated rind and juice of 2 limes
   30ml/2 tbsp sugar
   30ml/2 tbsp *tuk trey*
   2 green Thai chillies, seeded and
     finely sliced
   1 small bunch fresh coriander
     (cilantro), stalks removed,
     finely chopped
   salt

1 Peel, halve and stone (pit) the green mangoes, and slice them into thin strips.

2 In a bowl, mix together the lime rind and juice, sugar and *tuk trey*. Add the mango strips with the chillies and coriander. Add salt to taste and leave to stand for 20 minutes to allow the flavours to mingle before serving.

Per portion Energy 92Kcal/391kJ; Protein 1g; Carbohydrate 22g, of which sugars 15g; Fat 0g; Cholesterol 0mg; Calcium 32mg; Fibre 33g; Sodium 0.5g

BANANA BLOSSOM SALAD WITH PRAWNS

BANANA BLOSSOM IS VERY POPULAR — THE PURPLISH-PINK SHEATHS ARE USED FOR PRESENTATION, THE PETALS AS A GARNISH, AND THE POINTED, CREAMY YELLOW HEART IS TOSSED IN SALADS, WHERE IT IS COMBINED WITH LEFTOVER GRILLED CHICKEN OR PORK, STEAMED OR GRILLED PRAWNS, OR TOFU.

SERVES FOUR

INGREDIENTS
  2 banana blossom hearts
  juice of 1 lemon
  225g/8oz prawns (shrimp), cooked
    and shelled
  30ml/2 tbsp roasted peanuts, finely
    chopped, fresh basil leaves and
    lime slices, to garnish
For the dressing
  juice of 1 lime
  30ml/2 tbsp white rice vinegar
  60ml/4 tbsp *tuk trey*
  45ml/3 tbsp palm sugar
  3 red Thai chillies, seeded and
    finely sliced
  2 garlic cloves, peeled and finely
    chopped

2 To make the dressing, beat the lime juice, vinegar and *tuk trey* with the sugar in a small bowl, until it has dissolved. Stir in the chillies and garlic and set aside.

3 Drain the sliced banana blossom and put it in a bowl. Add the prawns and pour over the dressing. Toss well and garnish with the roasted peanuts, basil leaves and lime slices.

1 Cut the banana blossom hearts into quarters lengthways and then slice them very finely crosswise. To prevent them discolouring, tip the slices into a bowl of cold water mixed with the lemon juice and leave to soak for about 30 minutes.

COOK'S TIP
Banana blossom doesn't actually taste of banana. Instead, it is mildly tannic, similar to an unripe persimmon – a taste and texture that complements chillies, lime and the local fish sauce.

VARIATION
If you cannot find banana blossom hearts in Asian supermarkets, you can try this recipe with raw, or lightly steamed or roasted, fresh artichoke hearts.

Per portion Energy 103Kcal/438kJ; Protein 11g; Carbohydrate 15g, of which sugars 13g; Fat 0.5g, of which saturates 0.1g; Cholesterol 110mg; Calcium 54mg; Fibre 0.7g; Sodium 109mg

SOYA BEANSPROUT SALAD

HIGH IN PROTEIN AND FAT, SOYA BEANSPROUTS ARE PARTICULARLY FAVOURED IN CAMBODIA. UNLIKE MUNG BEANSPROUTS, THEY ARE SLIGHTLY POISONOUS WHEN RAW AND NEED TO BE PARBOILED BEFORE USING. TOSSED IN A SALAD, THEY ARE OFTEN EATEN WITH NOODLES AND RICE.

2 Bring a pan of salted water to the boil. Drop in the beansprouts and blanch for a minute only. Drain and refresh under cold water until cool. Drain again and put them into a clean dishtowel. Shake out the excess water.

3 Put the beansprouts into a bowl with the spring onions. Pour over the dressing and toss well. Garnish with coriander leaves and serve.

SERVES FOUR

INGREDIENTS
   450g/1lb fresh soya beansprouts
   2 spring onions (scallions), finely
     sliced
   1 small bunch fresh coriander
     (cilantro), stalks removed
For the dressing
   15ml/1 tbsp sesame oil
   30ml/2 tbsp *tuk trey*
   15ml/1 tbsp white rice vinegar
   10ml/2 tsp palm sugar
   1 red chilli, seeded and finely sliced
   15g/½oz fresh young root ginger,
     finely shredded

1 First make the dressing. In a bowl, beat the oil, *tuk trey* and rice vinegar with the sugar, until it dissolves. Stir in the chilli and ginger and leave to stand for 30 minutes to allow the flavours to develop.

Per portion Energy 76Kcal/317kJ; Protein 3.4g; Carbohydrate 8.6g, of which sugars 6.5g; Fat 3.3g, of which saturates 0.5g; Cholesterol 0mg; Calcium 27mg; Fibre 1.8g; Sodium 6mg

MARINATED FISH SALAD

SWEET-FLESHED FRESHWATER FISH AND SHELLFISH ARE OFTEN EATEN RAW IN CAMBODIA, PLUCKED STRAIGHT FROM THE WATER, OR TOSSED IN A MARINADE. WRAPPED IN A LETTUCE LEAF WITH EXTRA LEAFY HERBS, OR SERVED WITH NOODLES, THIS SALAD, KOY PA, IS LIGHT AND DELICIOUS.

SERVES FOUR TO SIX

INGREDIENTS
- 450g/1lb white fish fillets, boned and finely sliced
- juice of 4 limes
- 30ml/2 tbsp *tuk trey*
- 4 spring onions (scallions), finely sliced
- 2 garlic cloves, finely sliced
- 1 fresh red chilli, seeded and finely sliced
- 1 small bunch fresh coriander (cilantro), stalks removed
- lettuce leaves, to serve

1 Place the sliced fish in a large bowl. Pour over the juice of three limes and toss well, making sure all the fish is coated Cover and chill in the refrigerator for 24 hours.

2 Drain the fish and place in a clean bowl with the juice of the remaining lime, the *tuk trey*, spring onions, garlic, chilli and coriander. Toss well and serve with lettuce leaves.

Per portion Energy 66Kcal/280kJ; Protein 14g; Carbohydrate 1.2g, of which sugars 1.1g; Fat 0.6g, of which saturates 0.1g; Cholesterol 35mg; Calcium 11mg; Fibre 0.2g; Sodium 402mg

RAW BEEF SALAD WITH PEANUTS

THERE ARE MANY RECIPES FOR BEEF SALADS THROUGHOUT SOUTH-EAST ASIA, SUCH AS THE VIETNAMESE GOI BO, BUT THIS CAMBODIAN RECIPE, PLEAH SAIKO, IS QUITE DISTINCTIVE AS IT USES THE FLAVOURSOME FISH EXTRACT, TUK PRAHOC, AND ROASTED PEANUTS.

2 Meanwhile, in a small bowl, beat the remaining *tuk prahoc* with the juice of the third lime. Stir in the remaining sugar, until it dissolves, and put aside.

3 Put the beef slices, drained of any remaining liquid, in a clean bowl. Add the chilli, peanuts and coriander. Toss with the dressing, garnish with coriander leaves and serve immediately.

SERVES FOUR

INGREDIENTS
    45ml/3 tbsp *tuk prahoc*
    juice of 3 limes
    45ml/3 tbsp palm sugar
    2 lemon grass stalks, trimmed and
      finely sliced
    2 shallots, peeled and finely sliced
    2 garlic cloves, finely chopped
    450g/1lb beef fillet, very
      finely sliced
    1 red chilli, seeded and finely sliced
    50g/2oz roasted, unsalted peanuts,
      finely chopped or crushed
    1 small bunch fresh coriander
      (cilantro), finely chopped, plus extra
      leaves, to garnish

1 In a bowl, beat 30ml/2 tbsp *tuk prahoc* with the juice of two limes and 30ml/2 tbsp of the sugar, until the sugar has dissolved. Add the lemon grass, shallots and garlic and mix well. Toss in the slices of beef, cover and place in the refrigerator for 1–2 hours.

Per portion Energy 321Kcal/1343kJ; Protein 29g; Carbohydrate 15g, of which sugars 14g; Fat 16g, of which saturates 5g; Cholesterol 65mg; Calcium 48mg; Fibre 1.6g; Sodium 78mg

SEARED BEEF SALAD IN A LIME DRESSING

THIS IS A GREAT FAVOURITE IN CAMBODIA, VIETNAM AND THAILAND. IN CAMBODIA, IT IS MAINLY A RESTAURANT SPECIALITY, OR IT IS SERVED AS PART OF A FESTIVE SPREAD IN WEALTHY HOUSEHOLDS — BEEF IS EXPENSIVE AND DOES NOT PLAY A BIG ROLE IN THE DIET OF THE POORER RURAL COMMUNITIES.

SERVES FOUR

INGREDIENTS
  about 7.5ml/1½ tsp vegetable oil
  450g/1lb beef fillet, cut into steaks
    2.5cm/1in thick
  115g/4oz/½ cup beansprouts
  1 bunch each fresh basil and mint,
    stalks removed, leaves shredded
  1 lime, cut into slices, to serve
For the dressing
  grated and juice (about 80ml/3fl oz)
    of 2 limes
  30ml/2 tbsp *tuk trey*
  30ml/2 tbsp raw cane sugar
  2 garlic cloves, crushed
  2 lemon grass stalks, finely sliced
  2 red Serrano chillies, seeded and
    finely sliced

3 Drain the meat of any excess juice and transfer it to a wide serving bowl. Add the beansprouts and herbs and toss it all together. Serve with lime slices to squeeze over.

1 To make the dressing, beat the lime rind, juice and *tuk trey* in a bowl with the sugar, until the sugar dissolves. Stir in the garlic, lemon grass and chillies and set aside.

2 Pour a little oil into a heavy pan and rub it over the base with a piece of kitchen paper. Heat the pan and sear the steaks for 1–2 minutes each side. Transfer them to a board and leave to cool a little. Using a sharp knife, cut the meat into thin slices. Toss the slices in the dressing, cover and leave to marinate for 1–2 hours.

COOK'S TIP
It is worth buying an excellent-quality piece of tender fillet steak for this recipe as the meat is only just seared.

Per portion Energy 233Kcal/979kJ; Protein 26g; Carbohydrate 12g, of which sugars 9g; Fat 9g, of which saturates 3g; Cholesterol 69mg; Calcium 74mg; Fibre 0.5g; Sodium 400mg

CAMBODIAN HERBAL PASTE

THIS PASTE, KNOWN AS KROEUNG, COULD BE DESCRIBED AS THE ESSENCE OF CAMBODIA. LEMON GRASS, GALANGAL AND TURMERIC ARE THREE OF THE KEY FLAVOURS IN KHMER COOKING. THIS VERSATILE PASTE IS USED TO FLAVOUR MANY MARINADES, SOUPS AND STIR-FRIES.

MAKES ABOUT 150ML/¼ PINT/⅔ CUP

INGREDIENTS
    3 lemon grass stalks, trimmed, with
      outer leaves removed,
      and chopped
    25g/1oz galangal, peeled and chopped
    25g/1oz fresh turmeric, peeled
      and chopped
    8 garlic cloves, crushed
    1 small onion or 2 shallots,
      finely chopped
    4 kaffir lime leaves, ribs removed
    2.5ml/½ tsp sea salt

1 Using a mortar and pestle, grind the ingredients to a paste, adding a little water to bind. Or simply put all the ingredients in a food processor with 15–30ml/1–2 tbsp water and process until they form a paste.

2 Spoon the paste into a jar or small bowl and cover. Keep the *kroeung* in the refrigerator for up to a week.

Per portion Energy 25Kcal/105kJ; Protein 1g; Carbohydrate 5.2g, of which sugars 3.8g; Fat 0.2g, of which saturates 0g; Cholesterol 0mg; Calcium 36mg; Fibre 1.4g; Sodium 1014mg

TAMARIND DIPPING SAUCE

VARIATIONS OF THIS FRUITY DIPPING SAUCE ARE POPULAR WITH STEAMED OR GRILLED FISH AND SHELLFISH. THE COOKED FISH IS BROKEN INTO CHUNKS AND DIPPED INTO THE SAUCE.

MAKES ABOUT 175ML/6FL OZ/¾ CUP

INGREDIENTS
    30ml/2 tbsp tamarind concentrate
    2.5ml/½ tsp sugar
    15ml/1 tbsp *tuk trey*
    1 fresh red chilli, seeded and
      finely chopped

COOK'S TIP
If you find that the tamarind concentrate is too thick, thin it down with the juice of half a lemon rather than with water – this will ensure that you don't lose the trademark sour flavour of the tamarind.

1 In a small bowl blend the tamarind concentrate with 50ml/2fl oz/¼ cup water and the sugar. Stir in the *tuk trey* and most of the chilli. Garnish with the reserved chilli and serve.

Per portion Energy 61Kcal/257kJ; Protein 2g; Carbohydrate 13g, of which sugars 12g; Fat 0.6g, of which saturates 0.1g; Cholesterol 0mg; Calcium 15mg; Fibre 2.2g; Sodium 1074mg

NUOC LEO

VARIATIONS OF THIS POPULAR DIPPING SAUCE CAN BE FOUND THROUGHOUT VIETNAM, CAMBODIA AND THAILAND. ADJUST THE PROPORTIONS OF CHILLI, SUGAR OR LIQUID, ADDING MORE OR LESS ACCORDING TO TASTE. THIS IS GOOD SERVED WITH STEAMED, STIR-FRIED OR DEEP-FRIED VEGETABLES.

MAKES ABOUT 300ML/10FL OZ/2¼ CUPS

INGREDIENTS
  15ml/1 tbsp vegetable oil
  2 garlic cloves, finely chopped
  2 red Thai chillies, seeded
    and chopped
  115g/4oz/⅔ cup unsalted roasted
    peanuts, finely chopped
  150ml/¼ pint/⅔ cup chicken stock
  60ml/4 tbsp coconut milk
  15ml/1 tbsp hoisin sauce
  15ml/1 tbsp *tuk trey*
  15ml/1 tbsp sugar

1 Heat the oil in a small wok and stir in the garlic and chillies. Stir-fry until they begin to colour, then add all but 15ml/ 1 tbsp of the peanuts. Stir-fry for a few minutes until the oil from the peanuts begins to weep. Add the remaining ingredients and bring to the boil.

COOK'S TIP
This sauce will keep in the refrigerator for about one week.

2 Simmer until the sauce thickens and oil appears on the surface.

3 Garnish the sauce with the peanuts.

Per portion Energy 848Kcal/3525kJ; Protein 31g; Carbohydrate 39g, of which sugars 31g; Fat 64g, of which saturates 11g; Cholesterol 0mg; Calcium 104mg; Fibre 8g; Sodium 2498mg

TUK TREY DIPPING SAUCE

THERE ARE MANY VERSIONS OF THIS POPULAR CHILLI DIPPING SAUCE, VARYING IN DEGREES OF SWEETNESS, SOURNESS AND HEAT. SOME PEOPLE ADD RICE VINEGAR TO THE MIX.

MAKES ABOUT 200ML/7FL OZ/SCANT 1 CUP

INGREDIENTS
  4 garlic cloves, roughly chopped
  2 red Thai chillies, seeded and
    roughly chopped
  15ml/1 tbsp sugar
  juice of 1 lime
  60ml/4 tbsp *nuoc mam*
  2 tbsp unsalted peanuts

1 Using a mortar and pestle, pound the garlic with the chillies and sugar and grind to make a paste.

2 Squeeze in the lime juice, add the *nuoc mam* and then stir in 60–75ml/ 4–5 tbsp water to taste. Blend well. Beat in the peanuts to add texture.

Per portion Energy 140Kcal/593kJ; Protein 5.; Carbohydrate 30g, of which sugars 24g; Fat 0.4g, of which saturates 0.1g; Cholesterol 0mg; Calcium 30mg; Fibre 2.4g; Sodium 4277mg

SWEET SNACKS
& DRINKS

Juicy fruit and sweet snacks are enjoyed by all Cambodians.

Seasonal fruit includes mango, coconut, rambutan, durian,

mangosteen, starfruit, watermelon and bananas. Sweet snacks

such as Pumpkin Pudding in Banana Leaves and Golden

Threads are eaten throughout the day. Other sweet tastes include

ripe fruit, peeled and eaten or crushed into juice, and ice cream

made with the flesh of pungent durian. Alternatively, in a quiet

moment, try a Cassava Sweet with a cup of light Jasmine tea.

STICKY RICE ^{WITH} DURIAN SAUCE

THROUGHOUT SOUTH-EAST ASIA, PEOPLE ENJOY A SNACK OF SWEET STICKY RICE. EVERY CULTURE HAS THEIR OWN FAVOURITE VERSION OF THIS SNACK — SOME LIKE IT SERVED WITH SWEETENED RED BEANS, OTHERS WITH MANGO, AND THE CAMBODIANS EAT IT WITH A DOLLOP OF DURIAN SAUCE.

SERVES FOUR TO SIX

INGREDIENTS
   115g/4oz/generous ½ cup sticky
     glutinous rice, rinsed, and soaked in
     plenty of water for at least 6 hours
   550ml/18fl oz/2½ cups coconut milk
   30ml/2 tbsp palm sugar
   115g/4oz fresh durian flesh, puréed
   salt

1 Drain the sticky rice. Fill a wok a third of the way up with water. Fit a bamboo steamer into the wok and put the lid on. Bring the water to the boil, place a piece of dampened muslin (cheesecloth) over the bamboo rack and spoon the rice into it, leaving space all around for the steam to come through.

2 Carefully fold the muslin over the rice, cover the steamer, and steam for about 20 minutes, until the rice is translucent and tender but still has a bite to it.

3 In a heavy pan, heat the coconut milk with a pinch of salt and the sugar, until it has dissolved.

4 Beat in the puréed durian. Pour a little less than half of the mixture into a small pan and set aside. Add the cooked rice to the remaining mixture and mix well. Put the lid on the pan and simmer for a further 15 minutes. Divide the sweetened rice among individual bowls. Heat the reserved sauce in the small pan and pour it over the rice.

Per portion Energy 111Kcal/470kJ; Protein 2g; Carbohydrate 25.4g, of which sugars 10g; Fat 0.4g, of which saturates 0.2g; Cholesterol 0mg; Calcium 39mg; Fibre 0.2g; Sodium 101mg

COCONUT RICE PUDDING <u>WITH</u> PINEAPPLE

PERHAPS INSPIRED BY THE FRENCH, BAKED RICE PUDDINGS ARE POPULAR IN CAMBODIA AND ARE, GENERALLY, ACCOMPANIED BY FRUITS IN SYRUP, OR SAUTÉED BANANAS OR PINEAPPLE. THIS RECIPE REQUIRES LONG, SLOW COOKING IN A LOW OVEN, BUT IT IS WELL WORTH THE WAIT.

SERVES FOUR TO SIX

INGREDIENTS

  90g/3½oz/½ cup pudding rice
  600ml/1 pint/2½ cups
    coconut milk
  300ml/½ pint/1¼ cups full-fat
    (whole) milk
  75g/2¾oz/scant ½ cup caster
    (superfine) sugar
  25g/1oz/2 tbsp butter, plus extra
    for greasing
  45ml/3 tbsp grated fresh or
    desiccated (dry unsweetened
    shredded) coconut, toasted
  1 small, ripe pineapple
  30ml/2 tbsp sesame oil
  5cm/2in piece of fresh root ginger,
    peeled and grated
  shavings of toasted coconut,
    to garnish

2 After 30 minutes, take the dish out and gently stir in the toasted coconut. Return it to the oven for a further 1½ hours, or until almost all the milk is absorbed and a golden skin has formed on top of the pudding.

3 Using a sharp knife, peel the pineapple and remove the core, then cut the flesh into bitesize cubes.

4 Towards the end of the cooking time, heat the oil in a large wok or heavy pan. Stir in the ginger, stir-fry until the aroma is released, then add the pineapple cubes, turning them over to sear on both sides. Sprinkle with the remaining sugar and continue to cook until the pineapple is slightly caramelized.

5 Serve the pudding spooned into bowls and topped with the hot, caramelized pineapple and toasted coconut.

1 Preheat the oven to 150°C/300°F/ Gas 2. Grease an ovenproof dish. In a bowl, mix the rice with the coconut milk, milk and 50g/2oz/¼ cup of the sugar and pour it into the ovenproof dish. Dot pieces of butter over the top and place the dish in the oven.

VARIATIONS
The Cambodians and Vietnamese love sticky rice and mung bean puddings and always sprinkle a little extra sugar over the top to serve. You can also heat up a little sweetened coconut cream and pour it over the top. For a slightly different flavour, you could also serve the rice pudding with slices of seared mango or banana instead of the sautéed pineapple.

Per portion Energy 414Kcal/1735kJ; Protein 6g; Carbohydrate 56g, of which sugars 39g; Fat 19g, of which saturates 9g; Cholesterol 24mg; Calcium 156mg; Fibre 1.6g; Sodium 200mg

SWEET RICE DUMPLINGS IN GINGER SYRUP

OFTEN COOKED FOR THE VIETNAMESE TET CELEBRATION, THESE RICE DUMPLINGS ARE ALSO POPULAR IN CAMBODIA. THEY ARE FILLED WITH MUNG BEAN PASTE AND THEN SIMMERED IN A GINGER-INFUSED SYRUP. USING GLUTINOUS RICE FLOUR CREATES A SPRINGY, CHEWY TEXTURE.

SERVES FOUR TO SIX

INGREDIENTS
For the syrup
    25g/1oz fresh root ginger, peeled and
        finely shredded
    115g/4oz/generous ½ cup sugar
    400ml/14fl oz/1⅔ cups water
For the filling
    40g/1½oz dried split mung beans,
        soaked for 6 hours and drained
    25g/1oz/2 tbsp sugar
For the dough
    225g/8oz/2 cups sticky glutinous
        rice flour
    175ml/6fl oz/¾ cup boiling water

1 To make the syrup, stir the ginger and sugar in a heavy pan over a low heat, until the sugar begins to brown. Take the pan off the heat to stir in the water – it will bubble and spit. Return the pan to the heat and bring to the boil, stirring all the time. Reduce the heat and simmer for 5 minutes.

2 To make the filling, put the soaked mung beans in a pan with the sugar and pour in enough water to cover. Bring to the boil, stirring all the time until the sugar has dissolved. Reduce the heat and simmer for 15–20 minutes until the mung beans are soft – you may need to add more water if the beans are getting dry.

COOK'S TIP
These dumplings are popular at Vietnamese weddings. Coloured red with food dye, they represent good fortune.

3 Once soft enough and when all the water has been absorbed, pound to a smooth paste and leave to cool.

4 Using your fingers, pick up teaspoon-sized portions of the filling and roll them into small balls – there should be roughly 16–20.

5 To make the dough, put the flour in a bowl. Make a well in the centre and gradually pour in the water, drawing in the flour from the sides. Mix to form a dough, then cover and leave to stand until cool enough to handle. Dust a surface with flour and knead the dough for a few minutes, until soft, smooth and springy.

6 Divide the dough in half and roll each half into a sausage, about 25cm/10in long. Divide each sausage into 8–10 pieces, and roll each piece into a ball. Take a ball of dough and flatten it in the palm of your hand. Place a ball of the mung bean filling in the centre of the dough and seal it by pinching and rolling the dough. Repeat with the remaining balls.

7 Bring a deep pan of water to the boil. Drop in the filled dumplings and cook for a few minutes, until they rise to the surface. Once cooked, drain the dumplings in a colander. Heat the syrup in a heavy pan, drop in the cooked dumplings, and simmer for 2–3 minutes. Leave to cool and serve at room temperature, or chilled.

VARIATIONS
• For a spicy version, the syrup can be flavoured with a mixture of ginger, cloves, aniseed and cinnamon sticks.
• The dumplings can be filled with a sweetened purée of cooked sweet potato, mashed banana or even a mixture of chopped dried fruits.

Per portion Energy 231Kcal/975kJ; Protein 2.7g; Carbohydrate 54.7g, of which sugars 24.5g; Fat 0.3g, of which saturates 0g; Cholesterol 0mg; Calcium 23mg; Fibre 0.9g; Sodium 4mg.

PUMPKIN PUDDING IN BANANA LEAVES

NATIVE TO CAMBODIA, NOM L'POH IS A TRADITIONAL PUDDING THAT CAN BE MADE WITH SMALL, SWEET PUMPKINS, OR BUTTERNUT SQUASH. THIS IS A VERY MOREISH DESSERT, OR SNACK, WHICH CAN BE EATEN HOT, AT ROOM TEMPERATURE, OR COLD.

2 In a pan, heat the coconut milk with the sugar and a pinch of salt. Blend the tapioca starch with 15ml/1 tbsp water and 15ml/1 tbsp of the hot coconut milk. Add it to the coconut milk and beat well. Beat the mashed pumpkin into the coconut milk or, if using a blender, add the coconut milk to the pumpkin and purée together.

3 Spoon equal amounts of the pumpkin purée into the centre of each banana leaf square. Fold in the sides and thread a cocktail stick (toothpick) through the open ends to enclose the purée.

4 Fill the bottom third of a wok with water. Place a bamboo steamer on top. Place as many stuffed banana leaves as you can into the steamer, folded side up – you may have to cook them in batches. Cover the steamer and steam parcels for 15 minutes. Unwrap them and serve hot or cold.

SERVES SIX

INGREDIENTS
  1 small pumpkin, about 1.3kg/3lb,
    peeled, seeded and cubed
  250ml/8fl oz/1 cup coconut milk
  45ml/3 tbsp palm sugar
  15ml/1 tbsp tapioca starch
  12 banana leaves, cut into 15cm/6in
    squares
  salt

VARIATION
You can also try sweet potatoes, cassava or taro root in this recipe.

1 Bring a pan of salted water to the boil. Add the pumpkin flesh and cook for 15 minutes, or until tender. Drain and mash with a fork or purée in a blender.

Per portion Energy 60Kcal/257kJ; Protein 1g; Carbohydrate 13.6g, of which sugars 12.7g; Fat 0.5g, of which saturates 0.3g; Cholesterol 0mg; Calcium 64mg; Fibre 1.7g; Sodium 46mg

BAKED PUMPKIN <u>WITH</u> COCONUT CUSTARD

THIS IS A TRADITIONAL DESSERT FROM CAMBODIA AND THAILAND. ONCE THE CUSTARD-FILLED PUMPKIN IS BAKED, THE FLESH IS SCOOPED OUT WITH THE CUSTARD AND A HOT COCONUT SAUCE IS DRIZZLED OVER THE TOP. SWEET AND FRAGRANT, THIS IS SHEER INDULGENCE.

SERVES FOUR TO EIGHT

INGREDIENTS
    1 small pumpkin, about 1.3kg/3lb,
      halved, seeded and fibres removed
    400ml/14fl oz/1⅔ cups
      coconut milk
    3 large (US extra large) eggs
    45ml/3 tbsp palm sugar, plus a
      little extra for sprinkling
    salt
For the sauce
    250ml/8fl oz/1 cup coconut cream
    30ml/2 tbsp palm sugar

1 Preheat the oven to 180°C/350°F/ Gas 4. Place the pumpkin halves, skin side down, in a baking dish.

2 In a large bowl, whisk the coconut milk with a pinch of salt, the eggs and sugar, until the mixture is thick and smooth. Pour the custard into each pumpkin half and sprinkle a little extra sugar over the top of the custard and the rim of the pumpkin.

COOK'S TIP
Choose a small pumpkin as it will be more fragrant and less fibrous than a larger one.

VARIATION
This recipe can also be made with butternut or acorn squash and, interestingly, with halved avocados, mangoes and papayas, although the quantity of custard and cooking times may have to be adjusted.

3 Bake in the oven for 35–40 minutes. The pumpkin should feel tender when a skewer is inserted in it, and the custard should feel firm when lightly touched. If you like, you can brown the top further under the grill (broiler).

4 Just before serving, heat the coconut cream in a pan with a pinch of salt and the sugar. Scoop out servings of pumpkin flesh with the custard and place it in bowls. Pour a little sweetened coconut cream over the top to serve.

Per portion Energy 217Kcal/906kJ; Protein 4.5g; Carbohydrate 16g, of which sugars 16g; Fat 15g, of which saturates 12g; Cholesterol 71mg; Calcium 71mg; Fibre 1.3g; Sodium 88mg

DURIAN ICE CREAM

THE FRENCH LEFT A LEGACY OF ICE-CREAM MAKING IN THEIR COLONIAL TERRITORIES OF INDO-CHINA. ONE OF THE MOST UNUSUAL, AND YET SURPRISINGLY GOOD, ICE CREAMS IS MADE WITH THE POWERFULLY PUNGENT DURIAN, AND THIS IS VERY POPULAR IN CAMBODIA.

SERVES EIGHT

INGREDIENTS
    6 egg yolks
    115g/4oz/generous ½ cup caster
      (superfine) sugar
    500ml/17fl oz/2¼ cups full-fat
      (whole) milk
    350g/12oz durian flesh
    300ml/½ pint/1¼ cups double
      (heavy) cream

VARIATION
Other tropical fruits used to make ice cream include banana, mango and papaya, often spiked with lime zest.

1 In a bowl, whisk the egg yolks and sugar together until light and frothy. In a heavy pan, heat the milk to just below boiling point, then pour it slowly into the egg mixture, whisking constantly.

2 Strain the milk and egg mixture into a heavy pan and place it over the heat, stirring constantly, until it thickens and forms a creamy custard. Leave to cool.

3 Purée the durian flesh. Strain the custard into a bowl, then whisk in the cream. Fold in the durian flesh, making sure it is thoroughly combined.

4 Pour the mixture into an ice cream maker and churn until frozen. Alternatively, pour into a freezerproof container and freeze for 4 hours, beating twice with a fork or whisking with an electric mixer to break up the ice crystals.

COOK'S TIP
The sweet, creamy, yellow flesh of the strong-smelling fruit durian is delicious. The problem is getting to this nectar. With its tough, brownish skin covered in thorns, and the overwhelming smell as you cut into it, you might wonder if it's worth the effort. Be assured though – there is no doubt that it is. Just hold your nose and persevere.

Per portion Energy 392Kcal/1692kJ; Protein 32g; Carbohydrate 69g, of which sugars 32g; Fat 27g, of which saturates 15g; Cholesterol 211mg; Calcium 117mg; Fibre 0g; Sodium 40mg

CASSAVA SWEET

THIS TYPE OF SWEET AND STICKY SNACK IS USUALLY SERVED WITH A CUP OF LIGHT JASMINE TEA.
MORE LIKE AN INDIAN HELVA THAN A CAKE, THIS RECIPE CAN ALSO BE MADE USING SWEET POTATOES
OR YAMS IN PLACE OF THE CASSAVA.

SERVES SIX TO EIGHT

INGREDIENTS
  butter, for greasing
  350ml/12fl oz/1½ cups coconut milk
  115g/4oz/generous ½ cup palm sugar
  2.5ml/½ tsp ground aniseed
  salt
  675g/1½lb cassava root, peeled
    and coarsely grated

COOK'S TIP
To prepare the cassava for grating, use a
sharp knife to split the whole length of
the root and then carefully peel off the
skin. Simply grate the peeled root using
a coarse grater.

1 Preheat the oven to 190°C/375°F/
Gas 5 and grease a baking dish with
butter. In a bowl, whisk the coconut
milk with the palm sugar, ground
aniseed and a pinch of salt, until the
sugar has dissolved.

2 Beat the grated cassava root into the
coconut mixture and pour into the
greased baking dish. Place it in the
oven and bake for about 1 hour, or until
it is golden on top. Leave the sweet to
cool a little in the dish before serving
warm or at room temperature.

Per portion Energy 254Kcal/1086kJ; Protein 1g; Carbohydrate 64g, of which sugars 25g; Fat 1g, of which saturates 1g; Cholesterol 2mg; Calcium 39mg; Fibre 1.8g; Sodium 0.2g

GOLDEN THREADS

FREQUENTLY SOLD AS A SNACK IN THE STREET MARKETS OF CAMBODIA, THESE DELICATE GOLDEN THREADS, OR VAWEE, MADE FROM SUGAR, ROSE WATER AND EGG YOLKS, ARE ALSO USED IN RESTAURANTS AS A DECORATIVE GARNISH FOR SOME OF THE CUSTARDS AND RICE PUDDINGS.

SERVES TWO TO FOUR AS A SNACK

INGREDIENTS
    450ml/¾ pint/scant 2 cups water
    225g/8oz/generous 1 cup caster
        (superfine) sugar
    30ml/2 tbsp rose water
    12 egg yolks, lightly beaten together,
        and strained through a sieve

1 In a heavy pan, stir the water and sugar over a high heat, until the sugar dissolves. Bring to the boil, then reduce the heat and continue to stir for 5–10 minutes, until it begins to thicken. Add the rose water and continue to boil gently for 2–3 minutes. Pour the egg yolk into a piping (icing) bag with a single-hole nozzle, or use a jug (pitcher) with a narrow spout.

2 Carefully drip some of the egg yolk into the simmering syrup, moving backwards and forwards to form long threads or in a circular motion to form round ones. Cook the threads for about 30 seconds then, using a slotted spoon or chopsticks, lift them out of the syrup and on to a dish. Continue with the rest of the egg yolk, cooking in batches.

3 Serve the golden threads as a snack, or use them to garnish sweet rice dishes and fruit salads.

COOK'S TIPS
• Although considered a Thai speciality in Cambodia, these threads probably originated in India, or the Middle East, where traditional sweet threads and pastries are often poached, or soaked, in rose-scented syrup.
• It is important to keep the consistency of the syrup loose and flowing, not too thick, by adding more water if necessary while cooking the threads, which should be smooth. They may not be perfect on the first few occasions, as it takes a little practice to control the flow of the egg into the syrup, as well as lifting them out quickly while still golden.

Per portion Energy 1619Kcal/6811kJ; Protein 36g; Carbohydrate 235g, of which sugars 235g; Fat 66g, of which saturates 19g; Cholesterol 2419mg; Calcium 400mg; Fibre 0g; Sodium 122mg

SWEET SOYA MILK WITH PANDANUS

IN THE STREETS AND MARKETS OF CAMBODIA, FRESHLY MADE SOYA MILK IS SOLD DAILY. OFTEN INFUSED WITH PANDANUS LEAVES, OR GINGER, AND SERVED HOT OR CHILLED, IT IS A SWEET AND NOURISHING DRINK. IF YOU CAN'T FIND PANDANUS LEAVES, SUBSTITUTE THEM WITH A VANILLA POD.

MAKES 1.2 LITRES/2 PINTS/5 CUPS

INGREDIENTS
   225g/8oz/1¼ cups soya beans,
    soaked overnight and drained
   1.5 litres/2½ pints/6¼ cups water
   2 pandanus leaves, slightly bruised
   15ml/2 tbsp sugar

VARIATION
To make ginger-flavoured soya milk, stir in 25g/1oz grated ginger with the sugar. Bring the liquid to the boil and simmer for 10 minutes, then turn off the heat and leave to infuse for 20 minutes more.

1 Put a third of the soya beans into a blender with a third of the water. Blend until thick and smooth. Pour the purée into a bowl and repeat with the rest of the beans. Strain the purée through a fine sieve (strainer) to extract the milk. Discard the solids. Line the sieve with a piece of muslin (cheesecloth), then strain the milk again.

2 Pour the milk into a pan and bring it to the boil. Stir in the pandanus leaves with the sugar, until it has dissolved. Return the milk to the boil, reduce the heat and simmer for 10 minutes.

3 Remove the pandanus leaves, then ladle the hot milk into cups and serve, You can also leave it to cool, then chill in the refrigerator.

Per portion Energy 384Kcal/1584kJ; Protein 35g; Carbohydrate 9.g, of which sugars 9g; Fat 19g, of which saturates 4g; Cholesterol 0mg; Calcium 156mg; Fibre 0g; Sodium 384mg

SHOPPING INFORMATION

AUSTRALIA

Asian Supermarkets Pty Ltd
116 Charters Towers Road
Townsville QLD 4810
Tel: (07) 4772 3997

Duc Hung Long Asian
   Foodstore
95 The Crescent
Fairfield NSW 2165
Tel: (02) 9728 1092

Kongs Trading Pty Ltd
8 Kingscote Street
Kewdale WA 6105
Tel: (08) 9353 3380

Saigon Asian Food Retail
6 Cape Street
Dickson ACT 2602
Tel: (02) 6247 4251

The Spice and Herb Asian Shop
200 Old Cleveland road
Capalaba QLD 4157
Tel: (07) 3245 5300

Sydney Fish Market Pty Ltd
Cnr Pyrmont Bridge Road and
   Bank Street
Pyrmont NSW 2009
Tel: (02) 9660 1611

Burlington Supermarkets
Chinatown Mall
Fortitude Valley QLD 4006
Tel: (07) 3216 1828

CANADA

Dahl's Oriental Food
822 Broadview
Toronto, Ontario M4K 2P7
Tel: (416) 463-8109

Hong Kong Emporium
364 Young Street,
Toronto
Ontario M5B 1S5
Tel: (416) 977-3386

SOUTH AFRICA

Akhalwaya and Sons
Gillies Street, Burgersdorp
Johannesburg
Tel: (11) 838-1008

Kashmiri Spice Centre
95 Church Street
Mayfair, Johannesburg
Tel: (11)839-3883

Haribak and Sons Ltd
31 Pine Street
Durban
Tel: (31) 32-662

UNITED KINGDOM

Golden Gate Supermarket
16 Newport Place
London WC2H 7JS
Tel: 020 7437 6266

Loon Fung Supermarket
42–44 Gerrard Street
London W1V 7LP
Tel: 020 7437 7332

Rum Wong Supermarket
London Road
Guildford GU1 2AF
Tel: 01483 451568

Wing Tai
11a Aylesham Centre
Rye Lane
London SE15 5EW
Tel: 020 7635 0714

Wing Yip
395 Edgware Road
London NW2 6LN
Tel: 020 7450 0422
also at
Oldham Road
Ancoats
Manchester M4 5HU
Tel: 0161 832 3215
and
375 Nechells Park Road
Nechells
Birmingham B7 5NT
Tel: 0121 327 3838

Mail Order Companies
Fiddes Payne Herbs and
   Spices Ltd
Unit 3B, Thorpe Way, Banbury
Oxfordshire OX16 8XL
Tel: 01295 253 888

Seasoned Pioneers Ltd
101 Summers Road
Brunswick Business Park
Liverpool L3 4BJ
Tel: 0151 709 9330
www.seasonedpioneers.com

UNITED STATES

Asian Food Market
6450 Market Street
Upper Darby, PA 19082
Tel: (610) 352-4433

Asian Foods Ltd.
260–280 West Lehigh Avenue
Philadelphia, PA 19133
Tel: (215) 291-9500

Asian Market
2513 Stewart Avenue
Las Vegas, NV 89101
Tel: (702) 387-3373

Asian Market
18815 Eureka Road
South Gate, MI 48195
Fax: (734) 246-4795

Augusta Market Oriental Foods
2117 Martin Luther King Jr.
   Boulevard
Atlanta, GA 30901
Tel: (706) 722-4988

Bangkok Market
4757 Melrose Avenue
Los Angeles, CA 90029
Tel: (203) 662-7990

Bharati Food & Spice Center
6163 Reynolds Road Suite G
Morrow, GA 30340
Tel: (770) 961-9007

First Asian Food Center
3420 East Ponce De Leon Ave
Scottsdale, GA 30079
Tel: (404) 292-6508

Huy Fong Foods Inc.
5001 Earle Avenue
Rosemead, CA 91770
Tel: (626) 286-8328

Khanh Tam Oriental Market
4051 Buford Highway NE
Atlanta, GA 30345
Tel: (404) 728-0393

Oriental Grocery
11827 Del Amo Boulevard
Cerritos, CA 90701
Tel: (310) 924-1029

Oriental Market
670 Central Park Avenue
Yonkers, NY 10013
Tel: (212) 349-1979

The Oriental Pantry
423 Great Road
Acton, MA 01720
Tel: (978) 264-4576

Saigon Asian Market
10090 Central Avenue
Biloxi, MS 39532
Tel: (228) 392-8044

INDEX

AUTHOR'S ACKNOWLEDGEMENTS

In a book of this nature, there is always a great deal of research involved. For this I must mention the *Essentials of Asian Cuisine* by Corinne Trang, the most informative book on culinary cultures of South-east Asia; *South East Asian Food* by Rosemary Brissenden; and the excellent *Lonely Planet Guide to Cambodia.* On the ground, I would like to say a big thank you to Douglas Toidy and Le Huong at their Vung Tau fish farm, and to Peter Grant at Frank's, Singapore. And, I would like to thank the team at Anness Publishing Ltd.

PUBLISHER'S ACKNOWLEDGEMENTS

The publisher would like to thank Martin Brigdale for his photography shown throughout the book, with the exception of the following images:
t = top; b = bottom; r = right; l = left
Alamy pages 8b (Robert Harding Picture Library), 9b (World Religions Photo Library); Robert Harding Picture Library pages 6b, 9t; Superstock Ltd pages 7b, 8t; Travel-ink page 6t.